SKULL CATHEDRAL

A VESTIGIAL ANATOMY

ESSAYS

MELISSA WILEY

AUTUMN
HOUSE PRESS
PITTSBURGH, PA

SKULL CATHEDRAL: A VESTIGIAL ANATOMY
ESSAYS
An Autumn House Book

ISBN: 978-1-938769-56-6
1-938769-56-2
LCCN: 2019956231

"Autumn House Press" and "Autumn House" are registered trademarks owned by
Autumn House Press, a nonprofit corporation whose mission is the publication and
promotion of poetry and other fine literature.

Autumn House Press receives state arts funding
support through a grant from the Pennsylvania
Council on the Arts, a state agency funded by the
Commonwealth of Pennsylvania, and the
National Endowment for the Arts, a federal agency.

www.autumnhouse.org

FOR MELANIE

"Everything comes gradually and at its appointed hour."
—Ovid

CONTENTS

GRASPING
REFLEX

SWALLOWING NEEDLES

Closer to Honey

There
were gold veins on her ceiling. If not gold, amber then, something resembling resin. They once were blue, the same as everyone else's. Only so many years of sunlight filtering through smoke-stained curtains had altered their color, put light into the ceiling. Veins all the same. Someone hovering, then, above me. Someone whose inner wrists were all I could see of the body. Someone luminous, though not angelic. Not gone to heaven. Not waiting either. Never going.

My mom said the veins were only water damage from years of neglect to my grandmother's ceilings. She saw them fixing my attention as I lay on an old woman's bed, waiting to be taken home again. With my younger sister asleep beside me, I held my hands up to the ceiling, studied the differences in the webs woven beneath our skin, found my own too solid for any light to invade my bloodstream. Six or seven years old then, little as I knew about

3

the workings of the body, something inside me sensed my own veins could not turn golden until my life was also reaching its end. I half wanted to flood with light as well, half didn't.

I knew water alone, though, had not done this. We paid our ceilings at home little attention, did no more than my grandmother to keep them from falling. Still they were smooth, white, clean. Rain too was colorless. Water alone had not made veins once flowing with blood fill with something closer to honey. Water had not illumined what stretched out from a hidden heart toward the fingertips of someone clearly dying. Maybe my mom didn't mean to, but she was lying.

I was accustomed, though, to her missing things, those she didn't want to see, including my grandmother's dishes overflowing her sink, crusted with soft mounds of ketchup and mayonnaise that had begun to harden. My grandmother didn't dust her clock faces, didn't care to extend the life of her possessions, to clean them for even passing beauty. She filled her bathtub with dirty laundry, pants unraveling from their seams, blouses browned at their armpits that took her months to transfer to the washing machine. She never pasted wallpaper whose flesh was flaking back onto her walls more tightly. She did nothing with her days as far as I could determine beyond read Harlequin romances bought at the grocery, smoke cigarettes in bed, leaving their ashes to stain her sheets and pillowcases.

When my parents left us there on Saturday evenings, my sister and I had little to do in a house with so small of a yard attached, with no board games or Barbies. We sat beside my grandmother, sharing a cushion on her loveseat, watching Westerns where grizzled men shot each other off rickety saloon balconies. We went to bed early until our parents came, tucked a wool cover beneath our feet, in this way hoped for time to pass quickly. I say this of myself at least, because my sister still recalls time spent with our grandmother with fondness. In response, I only nod, keep silent.

4

Three years younger than me, she fell asleep more easily as I lay awake, resting my hands beneath my head, wondering how blood vessels could live their own life apart from the rest of the body. I shifted my gaze toward a dresser whose mirror was occluded with shoeboxes, whose drawers stuck when I tried pulling them open. Most were filled with photographs from times when my grandmother wore fur stoles and silk dresses, considered herself pretty. Others were empty.

Once my sister's breathing slowed into something sibilant and soothing, I turned on my side and regarded her eyelashes, deciding to ignore the life pulsing on the ceiling. Her eyelids revealed their veins' own fragile filigree, and I watched eyelashes long from the beginning lengthen even further into spider legs, growing restive, as my own eyes grew tired from staring. When I tried to pluck one or two of her lashes, when the pain woke her when I did, I told her I was trying to keep spiders from crawling into bed. To her, this made no difference.

She cried for my grandmother, who came always later than my sister wanted. Once she did, she gave my sister her wet kisses, overspread her half of the bed with a sour warmth, her tobacco breath. I was glad to escape this, to be less loved for being older, never the baby, for knowing better, as she said. As she straightened the cover over the edge of the bed, I studied my grandmother's movements, watched muscle sag from bone, detach itself from her skeleton. I felt this one life was not important, saw she had lived long enough already. When my parents came, I breathed them deeply in. I held my hand up to their chins, their smooth faces.

Chocolate Receding

LAST EVENING, I took a walk through a forest. In the slanting rain and wind, I walked back to my apartment from a gallery where a friend hosted a reception for a painting exhibition. I walked streets along which most trees have been razed to erect more buildings. Still, I walked on forest's bottom. The forest's ghost was present. It rose like smoke from soil long overlaid with concrete, while the trees have done the same as my grandmother I never loved has done before me. Dissolved back into the collective.

Carrying my umbrella, I trampled those few leaves fallen on the sidewalk into ochre ashes. I ran across an intersection, the asphalt gleaming. I ran because no cars would wait for me to cross more slowly, though my light was green. Going many times my speed, the cars were hurried as their drivers sat stationary. Those spindles of trees left growing between cracks in the concrete interlaced their branches into a wooden webbing.

My friend who held the exhibition paints nudes, mostly women, who as models are more forthcoming than men. Last night, though, she told me she has found a striking male specimen willing to pose for her through the coming winter. She touched him on the shoulder, introduced me. He told me his name in a voice little more than a murmur, when I felt a pain in the space behind my sternum. A quiet recognition. Someone I want to love even though I'm married, someone from whom life creates distance.

The space between my heart and sternum contracts each time this happens, the space where I'm forced to swallow another man whole again. The space where my heart might expand but doesn't, wanting to remain open. A space for beauty alone then, for movement. A space for beauty itself rather than a single image, which in time must vanish, become the ghost of a forest. Still my friend's muse looked at me with light shining through him. His skin glowed golden. Although he was young and handsome, his bloodstream was halfway turned to honey. I felt I could almost taste him.

I turned to talk to other friends, other artists, because I enjoy their conversation, because I have known since I was six or seven there is nothing you can keep here at forest's bottom, least of all another person, not even your own life, its pleasures and aversions. There was little reason to speak to him any longer, to ask him questions. Still the pain I felt when I glanced in his direction told me it would take some time to swallow him, to clear the space, keep it open.

As I was putting my coat on, tying my scarf around my neck, my friend hugged and thanked me for coming. Looking again toward the man she would soon paint naked, she said he had recently gone to see a doctor, had received a diagnosis he was still trying to process. Although he looked perfectly healthy, his blood tests had come back positive for a rare cancer, something malignant. He had been the one who asked her to paint him.

She said she met him only a few months ago, through another artist. I pulled my gloves from my pocket, and she confessed she was afraid she couldn't do him justice. She admitted, though, he told her again and again how much he enjoyed her way of translating bodies onto canvas. He wanted to be made into art that would outlive him, hung beside other nude women before he lost all his hair, grew too thin, wasted into nothing. I had no idea if the light shining through him was there before his illness. I half wished I could unsee it, half wished I couldn't.

I left and crossed the street, walked past a factory making bars of chocolate. A single rubber boot was frozen in a pond thinned into a shallow lake near the entrance. I crossed a bridge overarching a highway, when the smell of chocolate receding entered me with the force of a body. Once I passed the factory, it began to mix with pain made sharper from my friend's muse waving as I left, saying it was nice to meet me. The sweetness and cruelty of chocolate kept in a factory facing a gallery.

I had no reason to be as affected as I was by his diagnosis. Yet this dying back into the collective is easier to accept when all that leaves you is a forest, when the person is old and ugly, when a face you find chiseled and attractive has not looked into your own with a question, when you have not stared back with a knowing

7

that—although you are not someone he would notice were you not a friend of the artist—yes, you would keep him. Had you the option.

Edible Fuchsia Flowers

THE FIRST magician asked for volunteers from the audience. I pointed down at my sister's head when, smiling as he adjusted his glasses, the magician told me to come on stage instead. He said this was my punishment for volunteering someone who looked as unwilling as she did. Handing me his top hat, he asked me to confirm he'd hidden nothing inside it. I felt a small flap but nodded, did as he expected. As he performed his next trick, making cards disappear and reappear again, I continued palpating this same silk pocket. Before I came on stage, he'd produced several eggs from its crevice.

When I gave his hat back to him, I felt I knew something of his secret, felt he might have taken better care to conceal it. After asking the audience for silence, he pulled out a chick whose cheeps echoed down the hallway. His secret then became mysterious again, though the magician himself was balding, corpulent. He could birth a baby chick from a thin film of fabric, make life from something lifeless, but could never wound me with his beauty. I returned to my seat, when he chose a second then third assistant. I looked down at my hand, which had slipped inside the crevice from which things kept coming yet nothing was kept. I took a sip from my drink, and my sister whispered the act had been better with me in it.

Overhanging the rims of our cocktail glasses were edible fuchsia flowers. My sister and I ate their petals, their pistils, their stamens. Their taste was delicate, lingered. Fifteen minutes or so later when she mentioned the second magician was handsome, I purred and nodded. A man with tousled blond hair and square shoulders fanned his cards across a table overspread with velvet as

I shifted an earring fallen from a previous performance across the floor with my shoe flat. Sounding a plaintive music, I watched the veins roping his hands dilate with the rhythm. He shuffled his card deck as I sat with my legs crossed, my mouth half open.

His card tricks finished, he reached inside his vest and pulled out a series of needles strung together like paper dolls with thread. He turned toward the exit, allowing us to study his profile as well as his shadow's silhouette on the wall behind him. Each needle fell down his throat as if it were going to sew something together inside him, though the truth was the opposite. The truth was and always has been that needles are sharp things apt to wound softer organs. The best place for them to fall down a human body if they must do this is in the quiet place behind the sternum, where they can tear apart the stitches binding any image of any random person. The face dissolves, but beauty itself remains, keeps moving.

The magician swallowed nine or ten needles in as many seconds with the room gone silent. His muscles had developed the ability to loosen in response to the threat of pain, of suffering, the reverse of human instinct. His face blushed then reddened into something wrenching to witness. My sister squeezed her hands into fists, and gradually he pulled each one of the needles out by their thread again. Unlike the first magician, he needed no assistant.

A couple days after this, he stood in front of me at an intersection not far from my apartment. The light changed. He crisscrossed traffic while talking to another man who walked beside him. Pausing on the other side of the street, his eyes seemed to smile while the rest of his face held little expression. A play of light across his lips, his forehead, sharpened all his edges. A leather sky darkened against the milk of his skin, a smooth and silken surface. As he reached inside his pocket, I turned in the opposite direction. I wanted to follow him but kept my distance.

Whatever allowed him to swallow needles without bleeding his liver, his kidneys, all his viscera dry and lifeless, this had been the opposite of illusion. Unlike the first magician, he had simply surrendered to something unpleasant, called it magic. He had taught his esophagus to soften rather than contract in the face of pain that never came for this reason. The needles he swallowed were only an extension of what is possible when the whole body loosens. I believe this without knowing from experience.

Smoothened into Cream

OF THOSE old photographs once filling my grandmother's drawers and shoeboxes, of those my sister and I've kept, there are only a few taken from times I can remember, when veins filled with sunlight straggled across her ceiling. In one, remaining clearly in my memory, my grandmother sits on her loveseat holding my sister as a baby. I stand behind them on a cushion, smiling with my arms wrapped around my grandmother's neck. She doesn't seem to notice.

Her face evinces little awareness of how close I may be to strangling someone whose death two decades later will cause me no suffering, will not be a problem. Her gaze is fixed on the baby she nestles in her lap instead, while her forefinger is caught in my sister's grip. From the serenity of her expression, she seems to imagine my sister is holding onto her with love when love doesn't come into it. Although the photograph has yellowed with age, her finger still looks scarlet toward the tip.

When a finger, a strand of hair, a necklace is placed inside an infant's hand, it closes with a strength never replicated in the child, the adult, the adolescent. The instinct, known as the palmar grasp, lasts until the baby reaches five or six months of age. Afterward, it vanishes as if it had never been. Yet its brief appearance reflects, according to most scientists, our evolution from early primates who held onto their mothers' fur as infants while swinging through the canopy of a forest.

The grasp recalls memories of a fall so harrowing our hands have not forgotten. That we find ourselves at forest's bottom still seems strange to us as children. We look instead toward the sky, the ceiling. We search for life there, finding veins in what is only water damage, finding that beauty disappears on the ground too quickly. It takes some time for us to realize then begin accepting this is where life now happens. Yet the relaxing of the hand, the too easy letting go of objects, also reveals our bodies' wisdom. It is our muscles' recognition of our need now to dwell where streams empty into oceans, rivers debouch from mountains. Our need to soften.

For weeks, my grandmother's breathing sounded like a rusted lawnmower engine. The tumor where before only her brain had been was the size of an orange, one of the nurses said when she came into her room to record her heart rhythm. Waiting for my mom to come back from buying coffee from a machine down the hallway, I imagined the orange rind turning rotten, blackening and attracting insects. The nurse suggested I speak to my grandmother as though she were listening, to ignore the gears grinding in the space behind her sternum. I held her hand, felt her pickled skin slacken, told her next to nothing.

I was not with her when the lawnmower engine turned from something merely rusted into a wholly useless mechanism. My mom, though, had been. Padding back inside our kitchen, she sat across from where I was reading a magazine and drinking milky tea. She sighed then said in my grandmother's last breaths her blue eyes opened, radiant, though never fixed on any object. All her wrinkles then smoothened into cream. In her last breaths, my grandmother became young again, her skin luminous, silken. A dazzling, a beautiful woman.

My mom looked out toward the sun collapsing onto the horizon and said my grandmother was a woman born for a life of the senses. A life, then, wasted. My mom didn't add this to the end, but I knew it was the reason she gave herself for why her mother didn't do laundry more often, dust her clock faces. She had been waiting, even as an old woman, for beauty to stay stagnant, fill her emptiness, rather than dissolve into the collective, rot at forest's bottom. Over time, her disappointment hardened into depression. She had seen some beauty, felt pain from not having it, refused to swallow its fleeting expressions, keep a space open.

I also believed what my mom said she witnessed. I believe as much now as I did then that the body holds these kinds of surprises when it allows itself to loosen. Our muscles have so many more memories to draw from than the fear of falling from times when all the world was a forest. I knew my mom wanted to see the end of her own mother's life as tragic, yet because of the light that filled her veins and smoothed her skin, she couldn't. Something coming through then, something perceived by the senses. Seeing the gold flowing through the veins in the ceiling but never knowing what the gold is. Rain too is colorless. Rain alone does not do this.

Sky of Yeast

MY SISTER called me as I was walking through a conservatory not far from my apartment. Outside, light snow was falling. Inside the house with glass walls and ceilings were enough trees grown tall enough to form a canopy. My sister was baking bread as she was speaking, something she does most weekends, something she finds soothing and makes her house smell of yeast for days afterward. The aroma, however, never dissipates completely. Saturday always comes around again.

I thought of her vaulted ceiling overarching her living room and kitchen, of her infant daughter looking up from the floor where she lay gurgling. Some of the yeast inevitably escaped the bread and floated to the dark rafters and creamy plaster painted in between them. For my niece, the ceiling sufficed as cloudless heavens, a sky of yeast. My sister cleared her throat and told me she was going to have a mammogram next week, for pain she hadn't wanted to mention when she visited me last weekend, when we had seen the magic.

I was walking through a room of ferns, plants still too full of an ancient beauty to grow any petals, pistils, or stamens. Plants dating from the dinosaurs and that had outlived them. I sat down on a wooden bench after she said this. I ran my finger up and down the blade of a fern straying onto my lap from the breeze of a fan, its spores aligned neatly as pearls on string hung around the neck of a woman. Each time I ran my finger across it one direction, the leaf curled closer to me. It came closer yet also contracted, as if in pain, hiding something.

The evening before this, I had eaten with my husband at a restaurant where the food was warm and filling, the red leather booths framed with taxidermy. Throughout dinner, my husband's attention had seemed to stray, his eyes looking past me. It wasn't until we stood to leave that I noticed he had been facing an extremely beautiful woman seated behind me, looking my same direction. That he wanted to stare into her face and what he could see of her body, I recognized as only human, yet before my sister called this had continued to hurt me. I was aware he kept certain images hidden in the quiet place behind his sternum. A place that to each of us remains private.

As I rubbed the leaf of the fern the other direction, it unfolded, from dying to life again. In response to my silence, my sister explained the pain in her breast, occasional discharge even though she stopped breastfeeding months before this, could be other things than what we both were fearing. I curled my spine, sank lower on the bench, ran my finger across my eyelashes as a small spider scaled some stones beside me. I closed my eyes and saw the face of my friend's muse again, knowing nothing was permanent, only the continual parade of beautiful men and women. Far too many in one city to ever hope to see the same one again.

Before my sister mentioned her mammogram, I was going to tell her about seeing the handsome magician at the intersection, to ask her what were the chances without waiting for her to answer the question. Now it wasn't important. She had already forgotten him. I clenched my hand into a fist, released the air I was holding. As the muscles in my hands slackened, I realized I was fine with most people dissolving back into the collective. I knew so few of them. But not my sister, who has long forgotten I ever plucked spider legs growing from her eyelids, who loved my grandmother when I didn't. I walked outside, felt cooler air descending from a sky left cloudless and empty.

Half the Blackberries

THE EVENING I met my husband, in a bookstore café by accident, I was writing a paper for a class in metaphysics. At some point, he looked up from the book he was reading, asked me what I was writing. I smiled and told him the nature of existence, whether this life was real or wasn't. I smiled because I knew how vague this sounded, though soon he asked me my conclusion. I told him I was undecided, though if the answer was illusion, the body disagreed with this, maintained its own reality. We spoke for more than three hours as I remember it, until the café closed and we walked together to the train station then took the train in different directions.

Among the many topics we fell into that evening, one of the few he still recollects clearly is something I confessed I once did to my sister. I'm still unsure why I told this to someone who was a stranger to me. I only know that some part of me wanted him to know who I was at bottom. There was beauty in him, and I was too young to be conscious of the need to preserve a space for one face to dissolve so another can replace it, to allow for beauty's movement. I also wanted him to have an honest image of me, to take more time perhaps than he wanted to swallow and forget this young, uncertain woman.

Deep in southern Indiana, I told him, I as good as made my sister, no more than five or six years old then, climb to the top of my dad's tallest grain bin. I ordered her to climb a ladder higher than I ever had courage to climb myself, simply so I could see someone standing at its apex, a small figure filling some of our rural sky's emptiness. I wanted her, however briefly, to escape the forest's bottom. I told her I would never love her again if she didn't do it. I am fairly sure I meant this.

That afternoon, my grandmother was visiting, escaping the smallness of her yard so close to her neighbors, her Westerns, her water-damaged ceilings. She sat in the shade of our back porch, smoking cigarettes, while my mom picked blackberries growing from the fence lining our garden. My grandmother lazed in a lawn chair for hours, eating half the blackberries. Had she not been there, my mom would have filled more pies with them, made more jam to sweeten our toast at breakfast. My grandmother, though, didn't think about this, didn't wash her dishes.

I was pulling weeds deeper in the garden as our dog sat at her feet. I heard her ask my mom about my sister, about where she'd gone for what now seemed like ages. From the beds of cabbage I was hoeing, I shouted she was climbing the grain bin. I said this casually. To me, my sister was taking too long to reach its apex. Shortly after she started, I had gotten bored watching, was only waiting for her to finish.

My mom abandoned the blackberries and rushed to the base of the grain bin. My grandmother followed more slowly, mimicking her panic. I trailed yet more lazily behind them. My sister, almost at the ladder's tip, started crying once she saw she had an audience. She was wearing pink rubber thongs and complained her hands were starting to slip. I still have no idea if this was true or only what she feared might happen. But I saw the rungs were spaced at a wide distance for the length of her legs. She was likely tired, the sun high and bright in the heavens.

Brushing her hair back from her shoulders, my mom climbed up only to bring her down again, after which my sister fell into my grandmother's arms as if she were a baby. Had she let go while still on the ladder, had her grip weakened, she would have died, my grandmother said, nauseated, adding I should have known better than this. She had meant to punish me, but I knew my sister held on more tightly for this reason. I knew there was little danger yet of any of us falling.

HYMEN

A TRAVELING CIRCUS

She was nineteen the summer Federico Fellini met her at Fiumicino and helped to fold her legs inside his limousine. She looked out the darkened windows at the slipstream of taxis and confessed she held her purse to her bottom as she walked through customs. Making biscuits back in Indiana, slathering them with gravy, her grandmother warned her Italian men might try and pinch. Only with her hand-sewn dress fraying at its hem, with its print of white daisies unraveling, Sandy left the airport unmolested.

Stunned and sleepless, she'd forgotten the extent to which her size offered its own protection. Looking for Fellini, for someone stout and graying waving her to his side, she gripped her luggage with the hesitation of a much smaller woman alone in a country where she doesn't speak the language. This in itself was freeing, she realized long after her time in Italy dissolved into memory, this sense of being frozen in a warm and unfamiliar present. The only sensation that had ever approached it was wearing her first skirt of

19

the spring, sliding one leg past the other with only air between. As she stood waiting for the limousine, she felt her face loosen into something silken without being able to name the feeling.

Somewhere over the Atlantic, she had begun smelling of citrus. She thought at first it came from the air vents in the cabin. Later, she realized the aroma wafted from her own inner wrists. She knew this for certain only once she opened the shutter of a window too small to hold her face yet letting all the sky in. Though the plane landed in Rome safely, and on time no less, her legs wobbled when she left the jet bridge. She felt vaguely as if she could drop from a tree, as if while flying over Greenland she had shrunken into an orange or a lemon still hanging suspended. Weightless compared to what she'd been in Indianapolis, she felt someone had peeled her without her knowledge. She had been peeled but not yet fallen.

Crouched inside a car with leather seats stitched by Tuscan workmen, she thanked Fellini for making her accommodations. After scratching a bug bite on her neck, she let her hands rest in her lap a moment, then struggled to remove her sandals because her feet had swollen while flying across the ocean. Seeing this, Fellini bent over at his waist. For several minutes, his fingers wrestled with her left shoe's leather strap. Once the flap gave way, once the buckle opened, they laughed together at his easy exhaustion, at his cursing in Italian. On a mild late morning, he was visibly sweating.

They had needed this, however. They had needed some small struggle between them to mask his embarrassment at her reason for meeting a maestro, a man looking little different from other middle-aged men whose hair was thinning. Fellini had imported a giantess, the world's tallest woman, standing at seven feet, five inches and still growing. He had hired attendants from the Vatican to escort her to the set for a small part in *Fellini's Casanova*, a film of which I have seen only fragments, a film whose duration I doubt I'll ever witness if for no other reason than—for all Casanova's conquests, for all her own unwanted attention—Sandy herself remained loveless. After leaving Italy, she smelled of citrus for no reason.

And this Sandy Allen. She has never broken her hymen. Days later, this is what Fellini tells his producers in private when sitting on his terrace drinking cognac, when overlooking the Coliseum backlit in the distance. He thinks this to himself first inside his studio as the dwarfs he has brought back from a Sardinian vacation are adjusting their wigs, as he imagines each of their heads inserted between her legs—first their heads and then their stomachs—until even their feet are swallowed by her vulva's expanses. Each small man in his entirety, Fellini hyperbolizes, would still be too small a phallus to fill this woman with dark down lining her upper lip's peaks and central canyon.

More muscular than expected when shirtless, the two dwarfs when standing end to end still fail to match the length of Sandy. They say next to nothing in Fellini's script, only bathe her in one of two scenes in which her character, Angelina, makes an appearance. Casanova himself stays silent as he peers through a seam in her tent. His smile is toothless as he watches, as is that of his director behind him. Both smear their lips in a sickle across their faces.

Through serpentine alleys and recessed windows lined with succulents, more than a mile in the distance, Sandy cannot hear what Fellini is repeating then slurring in Italian over another glass of cognac. She has lived all her life without touching her finger to her hymen. She is still more child than woman, though Italy has already begun to change this, has begun but will not finish. She realizes she is the only woman in the film Casanova does not sleep with. She acknowledges she is here as spectacle alone. Still falling deeper into her bed's depression as her ankles wrestle themselves free from her sheet, she allows herself to think Italian is a language made for birthdays while knowing the thought is silly.

Each time she hears another incomprehensible sentence's rhythm, its laughing music, she imagines someone licking his fingers clean of icing. A week before she left Indiana, her grandmother sewed her a new dress looking like an apron with sleeves, leaving room for Sandy still to lengthen. The dress began fraying at its hem as soon as the plane landed in this new country. The print of daisies started wilting as her body seemed to lighten.

She wakes well before morning, when the world is still swathed in darkness. She opens her window's curtains and looks out over the Pantheon, observing its dark oculus from her higher vantage, its hole through which rain cools the building. She sees the eye that itself sees nothing and hears a couple on the other side of the wall. It is the first time she has heard the quickened breathing, the cries of panic followed by a softer silence. She holds her own breath and remembers her body's size offers its own protection against pinching. She fills a glass with water from the bathroom sink, knowing that with each new birthday she is still growing. And though she cannot hear what Fellini is saying closer to the Coliseum—though she has never thought about the blood that will flow from her hymen if it's ever broken—still she catches some of the phrase's music. His mocking filters into her fitful dreaming in a time zone to which she never adapts completely before the time comes to leave.

Years later, Sandy will become a sideshow attraction in the Guinness World Records Museum near Niagara Falls. Later yet, she will work as a secretary in Indianapolis, where she will be grateful simply to make a living, to have money to pay for groceries, for slim slices of cheese she'll melt over bread nearly every evening. Eventually, she will all but have forgotten Italy. Her face will slacken into something silken only in sleep. She will die in 2008 at the age of fifty-three, a few years after my paternal grandmother has likewise stopped breathing, only a few doors down in the same home of convalescence without the two ever meeting. Before both meet their end, they will do little more than spoon themselves canned peaches off of plastic trays. They'll take turns walking with the same nurses' aides down the same hallways. Lying flat in their beds, they will both press plastic buttons on a remote control when a channel grows snowy with static.

I never glimpsed Sandy in the building's entrance, where daytime programs were rebroadcast more loudly in the evening. Only after my grandmother was buried did my father mention Sandy was still there, still barely living, something he'd gathered from a nurse on a smoke break. I visited my grandmother there only twice before she succumbed to a minor illness. Both times I left quickly.

At her wake, I looked past her skin stretched flat across her cheeks and cast my gaze into the casket's amber varnish, where I found my own reflection. I confronted a young woman whose beauty was still more felt than seen, something I hoped might be changing. I told myself I would not die in a place this ugly, the same as all my family, the same as Sandy. In Chicago where I was pursuing graduate studies, a city with too large a population for everyone to have always known me, I had recently discovered love came freely from strange men in passing for women no taller, no shorter, no prettier than average, love that of all places is most forthcoming in Italy. A couple years before, I had been there to study.

Closing her window's curtains as Fellini grows yet drunker on his terrace, as he puts a napkin to his mouth and acts as if he is talking through her hymen, Sandy goes back to bed. She closes her eyes and lies awake with her knees tucked into her chest. She lies like a fetus who might be growing inside another giant, someone whose growth is expected. As she falls again unconscious, she tells herself Italian is a language of more than birthdays. She remembers how people whisper when she walks past them, when she stops to drink water from an ancient fountain. She knows here she is both wanted and unwanted, and the former to her is strange. It has been since the beginning, when her mother, an alcoholic, abandoned her to her grandmother's custody, so the only touch she has known has come from the elderly. The only touch that has come voluntarily within memory.

Within the next few days, she signs her autograph several times in her hotel lobby. Waiters place patches of linen over her lap as she eats outdoors in the heat, something she has done before only at picnics. Men with mustaches resembling blackened caterpillars set napkins so gently across her upper legs that she feels she is being put to sleep with a small blanket. They protect a part of her body, one her table has already hidden, with a white swath of fabric while her mind lapses into dreaming, into fantasies that she need never go home again, can keep traveling. So shy at school she sat always in the back of class, making vain attempts to vanish, she has come to Italy only to loom larger than she does already. She cannot escape, cannot become the same as any other tourist. She can only wash her bread in the juice of olives. She can have her eyelids painted by an artist whose name will roll through the closing credits.

For the scene in which Casanova spies her bathing, Fellini wants her topless. He does not tell her this, however, until filming begins, when Sandy insists on wearing a silk wrap the color of her skin, on being bathed in something she can show her grandmother without her ears turning scarlet, though they will change color regardless. More stubborn than Fellini anticipated, she smiles on screen without baring her teeth as she receives her ablutions. The scene begins and ends with the camera's close attention to a cluster of china dolls she plays with as if she were a child of six or seven. The character she portrays, Angelina, travels with a circus.

Only seconds before this scene begins, one of the dwarfs signals to Casanova that this is his chance to see Angelina naked. Wearing a wig dyed onyx, Sandy sits, gentle and impassive, as the dwarf, aware of Casanova's surveillance, begins to relish himself being examined. His eyes sparkle as he hops inside a wooden tub, as he hints by his expression that he himself has begun wondering whether Casanova or the director behind him is the true voyeur. Only Sandy sees no difference because Casanova died centuries before this, because Fellini's version of him is all that matters once the film is finished. Both dwarfs lightly splash, then kiss, Sandy's wrists. A long pause elapses as they sit lulled by tuneless music.

After she takes off her wig, after Fellini says they have done their final take, Sandy drinks her first glass of wine in Roman Polanski's mansion for a party she leaves alone and early. In the director's water closet before Fellini calls her limousine, she gropes for but cannot find the light switch, which lies just outside the room she locked as she went in. It is a fact of European life she has already forgotten. She bumps her head against a lamp above a mirror where she cannot see her face's reflection.

Inside her hotel room not long afterward, she undresses beside the toilet because she knows people have watched her enter. She knows they may be looking through her curtains from the piazza's fountain. In another mirror, she sees a gash across her forehead and soundlessly laughs at her clumsiness. She shifts her weight, feels the bidet sweat against her calf, and tells herself this is what comes of being drunken. She hears the couple on the other side of the wall making love again as Fellini confides to Polanski back inside his mansion that he has signed another actress to read Sandy's portion of the script. He will dub the voice of someone shaped into a violin over the sounds of what he finds too mannish.

Later still, Fellini will reveal to him and several other friends that the main reason he cast Donald Sutherland as his lead was because he resembles an erection. Casanova punctured one hymen after another according to the autobiography from which Fellini's script is adapted, making this reason valid. Again and again, he stabbed through this skin without thinking how little he in truth accomplished, if only because his own pleasure always took precedence, if only because the hymen itself serves no purpose. This tissue from which nothing new ever breaks but is only broken.

When I think of Casanova, when I think of Sandy Allen, whom he never ravished, I find myself wanting to believe Italy rescued her when I know it didn't, when there was never any lasting transformation. She had no choice except to die in the town I was born in, a place where I have no more funerals to attend and so will never visit again. There are so many more sidelong glances to be found in larger places, where love is often less gotten than glimpsed. I often still fall deeply into the delusion that beautiful places can make you beautiful with them, freeing you from the lovelessness that small towns can enlarge out of proportion.

Before he spies Angelina undressing, Casanova arm wrestles her in a tavern. He wrestles and loses, then follows her as she remains unaware of his movements, as she wears a white veil that to Fellini becomes a monstrous hymen, a vaginal membrane overspreading the whole woman. Once she enters her tent, she drops this. Now nearly naked, she reveals the expanses that people normally pay to witness, the enormity of flesh allowing her to be part of a circus traveling through Venice. Whether Sandy Allen wanted to continue being Angelina after she left Italy I can never be certain. I do believe there are worse things, however, than becoming a sideshow virgin. Worse than proceeding through Europe with a circus, of sleeping always in a tent, is staying in a Midwestern town so small it allows little room for movement.

There must be pleasure too to be gotten from holding your purse to your bottom as you walk through customs, from the illusion you are having your transformation. There is something to be said for drinking wine with Fellini, who glimpsed her body's bare topography through the keyhole of her dressing room without ever wanting to pinch any part of it. Even if Sandy's later life was not changed by Italy, she still walked through the streets of a city smelling of oranges before she left it for somewhere that had grown even uglier in comparison. Worse than being bathed by dwarfs for the lurid pleasure of a man resembling an erection is never having silk wrapped around your abdomen as the warmth of bathwater dissolves you into the weightlessness you have long imagined.

AND THOUGH she's dead now and all her traveling is finished, I still pretend I am waving silk flags across a field to her on occasion. I am speaking in semaphore to Sandy because we have long needed our private language, because the town where she died and I was born is bordered by fields of corn and soybeans, making the brightness of our flags loom all the starker against their autumnal brownness. No taller, no shorter, no prettier than average, I still sometimes think Sandy alone would have listened could we have only found enough silk to make our flags with—silk because these are the kind of wings we would have sprouted had we only returned from Italy different, freed of our chrysalises. And what could these flags have said? What would I have signaled to her and she waved back? That "I live here unnoticed" while she said the opposite. "I feel all but loveless," we would have waved to each other, in unison.

For a moment, as the dwarfs kissed her wrists, Sandy felt herself fill with beauty and knew it was preposterous. No man would kiss her lips except to tell his friends, except to fulfill a drunken challenge. Still looking out over a hill covered by cypresses, she realized it was the feeling she had needed without knowing it. The feeling alone was freedom.

Sandy Allen lived twenty-five years longer than expected, a fact my father mentioned when he read her obituary in the local paper. She lived with a heart twice as large as anyone else's, while no doctor had foreseen her living past age thirty. In later years, though, she suffered from severe depression. Her melancholy deepened as she developed arthritis and her movements became more restricted. If she had flags to wave while communicating with me in our private language, her shoulders would have popped painfully in their sockets. Had she tried to confess something, relieving her own lovelessness, she might have become even sooner silent.

By the time *Fellini's Casanova* premiered in the 1970s, hundreds of years had passed since Italy had seen its last traveling circus, a word meaning *circle* in Latin, a word denoting wholeness. Casanova famously escaped a Venetian prison after being sentenced to death for witchcraft during the eighteenth century, after trying to become an alchemist and practicing dark magic, after endeavoring to turn base metals into gold and failing. Yet alchemists only attempt to speed a process already in progress. Even stones eventually undergo transformation, sparkling and turning translucent, given enough time, given ages. And a circle by definition remains unbroken. A woman goes on living even after she has left the circus. Sometimes one life too is not enough for metamorphosis. Sometimes you surrender to the feeling of beauty knowing the feeling is fleeting.

Women who have had and not had their hymens broken may not all glimpse love from men in passing, but their hearts still beat like living lumps of jelly, a sign they are pupating—they are waiting—instead of doing what others might call real living. Tightly contained inside their skin, at times they feel as if they are decaying, though this long life of dying is necessary. It is what is needed for them to become something else to which they now bear no resemblance. Only once they emerge from their chrysalises, they don't brandish their dazzling wings by day, don't bother sucking all their nectar before sunset. Instead, they are moths drawn to flames, black and winged creatures of the evening. They breed in corners. Their larvae eat holes through clothing.

According to Chinese legend, Empress Leizu sat sipping tea under a mulberry tree when a cocoon fell into her cup and began unraveling. Its threads shimmered as the scalded pupa fell lifeless to cup's bottom. Meanwhile the threads continued to brighten as the empress began twisting them around her ankle into a bracelet. Making her face into a moue so she looked more attractive, she told her husband she wanted more of the filaments, and for several centuries afterward the Chinese carefully guarded their method of silk production. The industry flourished for the sake of women who enjoyed the feeling of the fabric next to their skin. Men's hands then became even rougher in comparison.

Silkworms as a species are no longer extant in the wild but have become completely domesticated. They exist only as caterpillars engaged in a process we interrupt to our own advantage. Silk harvesting relies on boiling water to kill the pupae, replicating what originally happened with the empress by accident. The caterpillar is now valued solely for its chrysalis, for its place of hiding before its moth wings ever develop. As a result, roughly 2,500 caterpillars die for every pound of fabric.

AFTER SHUTTING off all the lights in her hotel room and opening the shutters to starlight streaming through the Pantheon's oculus, after washing her face with soap made with milk strained from almonds, Sandy feels something inside her throbbing. She becomes conscious of a lifetime of loneliness now flown to Italy to keep her company. Fellini has finished filming not just her few scenes, but the entire movie.

What has lain dormant for several weeks now begins to yawn and stretch within her. It asserts its own life again somewhere inside her ribs, though she tries to hush it. Pulsing in the night when her grandmother on the other side of the ocean has only awakened, it is the same loneliness that has been with her as long as she remembers, the closest she will ever come to carrying a baby, a child she will be pregnant with always. Only here she senses what she has come to think of as her own kind of larvae, this sterling isolation, briefly bathed in beauty. This familiar pained life inside her is becoming. Maybe when she returns home she will look different, she thinks to herself while knowing the thought is silly. Maybe all those who have always known her, who have seen her grow so much larger than necessary, will recognize someone who now appears to be no taller, no shorter, no prettier than average. Fellini had told her she looked best in profile when she was pouting.

Even while being served tomatoes sliced and arranged in a star configuration next morning at breakfast, Sandy tries to imagine inhabiting her old life again, tries to imagine she doesn't mind it. She tries to resign herself to its ugliness by pretending there is no value in a traveling circus, pretending Angelina is not freer than her audience, who must return to their own walls and windows framed with curtains while she lives in a tent. For the time it takes

Sandy to finish one of her last meals in Italy, she pretends there is no such thing as wholeness. She pretends but cannot do it while tasting the juice of olives, while only an hour later men will offer her roses as she sits on Spanish steps she knows cannot be Spanish. She has found herself to be almost too good an actress. The circus has traveled through her but left too quickly.

THE LAST time I visited Rome was with my husband, who had never been before and found the city smaller than expected. Rain was streaming through the Pantheon's oculus when we walked inside, flooding the floor's marble center and then draining toward the edge of the building. We recorded a small film of it, but the rain falling through this slim cylinder, this eye that sees nothing, was quickly occluded by all the other tourists. At a nearby pizzeria, we were later seated beneath the edge of the awning so my husband's right shoulder and my left were both being soaked continuously. We inched our table closer toward four Norwegians, who asked if we minded taking their picture. The small patio was bordered by orange trees waving inside terracotta planters. The rain and steam released by the Roman heat opened the oranges' pores so that even the red wine we ordered tasted of citrus.

All were professors at the same college. They looked to be in their later sixties or early seventies and spoke perfect English. The two seated beside my husband were spouses, and those to my right were widowed, they offered, when I made the wrong assumption. The man sitting next to me had spent his life teaching Proust and other French poets, and his bottom lip was bleeding from the smallest of cuts to it. Food kept spilling out his mouth's right side as he talked to me, and there was an ugliness not to him as a person, but to the decay that comes with aging.

I forced myself to look into his blue eyes directly in order to keep from looking away. Though most of his eyelashes had fallen from his face, never to grow again, I found the light of recognition once I kept my gaze steady. Long after our meals were finished, long after my husband and the others had exhausted their topics of conversation, the two of us continued talking, of what exactly I have now forgotten. I only remember that, despite the differences in our ages, despite the fact I was young by comparison, I soon grew conscious neither one of us were as we seemed. We were both pupating. We would need another life for anyone to see us clearly.

I was seven when Sandy, then thirty-one or thirty-two, had grown even taller than while filming her part in Italy by a couple of inches. It was the only time I ever saw her in person. She had reached an age past which no doctor predicted her to live, and somewhere in the back of her mind she likely thought she was dying. She never saw me standing in line waiting to ride the same small roller coaster she had left, smiling and dizzy after letting the ride carry her over what later felt to me like the gusting waves of a tsunami. I said nothing, either to her or to my younger sister standing beside me then. I only noticed that the teeth she could not help baring were yellowed and spaced apart, none of them touching.

Wrapped tightly in my chrysalis, I had no desire to leave its warmth yet. Still cocooned deeply in the threads of childhood contentment, I could not imagine we would ever have anything in common. The prospect of my innocence unraveling, of ever wanting more than I was given, would have never occurred to me while the roller coaster still held its promise and I had yet to grow as dizzy as Sandy. I would still need years of living to grow heavy with waiting, with wanting more than I now know can often be expected of a single lifetime. For every living thing, you cannot expect fulfillment. Some moths must die as caterpillars simply so empresses can wear the threads they spend their lives spinning only to enable a metamorphosis that never happens. Some people must travel with circuses while others can only watch the performances, never leaving the towns where they were born. Wanting often has nothing to do with what happens. Ask the silkworm. Ask Sandy Allen.

APPENDIX

A RIVER HOMING

Sometimes when trying to fall asleep, when trying and failing, I tell myself a story of how the world ends. At different times and with different versions, I recount this narrative as a way of taking solace. Reminding myself of our world's dissolution—the disappearance of glaciers and forests, the rising incidence of mudslides and hurricanes—I find some consonance, a cosmic consolation for my own life's losses. Even mudslides, in other words, can offer salvation. In one of my favorite iterations of this story—one I have told myself so often that I now have difficulty believing it will not come to pass—until the mudslides come to save them, most of humanity has lived out their existence while feeling their real lives have not yet started. They have forgotten they are moving water themselves in essence, making their lives feel stagnant while proving all too fleeting. As each person progresses through each day while privately waiting for more to happen than ever does, most spend their weekends playing cards on their back porches, drinking beer while watching

TV. Weekday mornings, they slurp coffee as their cars stall in traffic. Meanwhile the rains have begun falling unabated.

Before a deeper awareness has a chance to manifest, the floods force their houses to slide away from their foundations, their drainpipes to deliquesce into river basins. Their homes go the way of all those living inside them, including their lips and knees and tendons. Their tracheas and tongues also flow downriver with the current, allowing no one to voice their panic as even their bones dissolve into primordial softness. Because life always comes from lifelessness, once the mudslides have ended and all of humanity vanished, the earth expands into a lusher roundness. With no more buildings left to press upon her surface, the planet breathes more deeply while restored to calmness. Gradually the earth reveals fresh continents as her shallower bodies of water recede beneath the stare of the sun. She exhales clouds whose rain leads bedrock, still supple and porous, to collapse in places. As more time spent in a lavish solitude passes, rain continues collecting in these depressions until these sunken pools of water eventually lengthen into underground rivers that come to resemble the earth's own liquid intestines.

FOR AS often as I tell myself how the world ends, for as comfortable as I have gotten with cataclysm, most of life fails to be this dramatic. Most endings arrive so gradually that we hardly notice. Most of life consists of minor disruptions, of almost imperceptible fissures in what most of us can be forgiven for taking as a wholeness. A couple weeks ago, I visited my sister and her family in southern Indiana, only a twenty-minute drive from the farm where she and I once lived with our parents. A thunderstorm on Friday in the early evening caused a power outage that lasted until late into the afternoon on Sunday, until only an hour after I left them. The outage was something I often used to experience when I too lived in the country, though this one persisted for longer than normal, throughout the two days and evenings I spent in the company of my only family apart from my husband. We grilled frozen pizzas in the yard instead of using the oven. In place of my sister's typical omelets for breakfast, we ate peanut butter sandwiches.

Soon after the storm ended on Friday, when we both still assumed electricity would be restored by morning, I helped my sister put her two young children to bed, singing softly and smoothing their foreheads. In the living room after we left them to their dreaming, my sister lit a candle, crossed her legs on her couch, and began reminiscing about the time we had once spent four days in the Yucatán with our parents, on a winter break when we both were still in college. As the last of the sunlight filtering into her living room was fading, as the candle on her end table burned more brightly in contrast, through the air in front of her she started tracing the stalactites she remembered hanging from the ceiling of a cave with blue water stirring at its bottom. She said she wished she could return to that place, to the one cenote our tour included, to that entrance to a series of underground rivers teeming with their own fish and aquatic plant species. She sighed and expressed her desire again to once more go swimming among them, this time bringing her husband and children.

As she spoke, I tried to summon her visceral sense of what the ancient Mayans called "ts'onot," meaning sacred well, or source of life's essence. I tried but realized I couldn't, especially when I felt myself becoming thirsty and wanted to pour myself a glass of water from the tap but knew this would be fruitless. In addition to powering all of my sister's appliances, electricity is needed to pump water from her well inside her home, which lies a few miles outside the nearest town's limits. For as long as the outage lasted, we had no water for washing our hands or showering, none to flush the toilets. Inside the refrigerator, which was slowly warming, there were a couple cartons of lemonade to keep us from dehydrating.

Instead of drinking either the lemonade or glass of wine her husband offered me, I went to bed early. I used the light on my phone to find my way upstairs as I left them both in the darkness. I changed into my nightgown and folded myself inside the guest bed. Knowing I would be unable to fall asleep for hours to come, I wriggled my feet free of the sheet and, lying supine while slowing my breathing, I tried to feel the stream of energy that is always pulsing through me, with or without my recognition, an underground river that, whenever I take time to pay it some attention, briefly carries me someplace timeless, making everything else of less consequence. My body heats with its warmth whenever I feel its presence. Though I fail to do so on a regular basis, this is also as close as I ever come to broaching transcendence. In these moments, I tell myself I am homing, the same as a pigeon, a sea turtle, a salmon. I tell myself I am returning to my origins, to life's very essence, even if the feeling usually lasts for only a few seconds.

I STILL remember on our first morning in Mexico when I was a senior in college, my sister a freshman, being the first one down to breakfast. Within another ten minutes, the manager of our hotel sat down at our table beside my parents. Though the smallness of the inn where we were staying seemed to have made this a custom, I was struck by his ease inside his body as he spread his hands and shoulder blades in the chair across from me. His skin looked too pale, his eyes too bluish, for him to have been born here, I imagined, and his American accent confirmed this. After a few moments of silence as he flattened a ripple of butter across a muffin, I asked him what had brought him here. He paused before he answered, and I registered the slight shock on my parents' faces. I felt their fear of my boldness in asking a stranger a personal question.

Leaning back in his seat, he smiled while admitting he had come here for his honeymoon several years ago. After his divorce, he returned less from sentiment than for the people, the climate. He came back for a cleansing of spirit and said he simply found himself unable to leave again. Here, he felt alive in a way he didn't other places. I watched his face as he said this, when I sensed less sadness than embarrassment, as if this hotel or region strewn with Mayan ruins were another woman for whom he had lusted throughout his marriage.

Leaving my sister and parents to continue the conversation, I stood to refill my coffee. While my cup was still empty, I helped a young boy to hold his plate level with the floor in order to keep the food he had piled on it from spilling. As I walked back to where my family was sitting, I detected the manager observing me. He leaned in closer to my parents and told them their oldest daughter was a sensitive person. I looked into his eyes after he said this and thought I saw a lonely light there shining. I felt almost certain he had never remarried. I also felt he had seen me clearly, though once more I saw some slight alarm overspread my parents' faces. I believe they were afraid of what this divorced man noticed. They were likely afraid of what, since I had grown used to living away from them, I might have revealed to strangers in public. By the end of breakfast, they had also bought the tour of the Mayan pyramids and cenote the manager recommended.

That afternoon, after our guide closed the door of his van outside the cenote's entrance, my mom, sister, and I changed into our bathing suits inside a restroom where none of the toilets had been flushed for unknown reasons. Either some woman or some women had heavily menstruated inside each stall and left us the evidence. Some woman or some women, now likely swimming in the same underground waters in which we would soon immerse ourselves, had made us witness the offal of their unfertilized eggs. The odor wafting from the stalls punished our senses. We changed as quickly as we could. We held our noses.

Outside the restroom, we waved to my dad and then stood in line behind him to jump off an enormous outcropping of granite. We leapt with reluctance into the water in which our guide had given us no real time to swim, only enough to scull over to the ladder before drying ourselves off again. With our guide watching us with his arms folded, we each stepped off the glittering rock with our bodies stiffened against the water's serene, reflective surface. My dad jumped first and emerged ten seconds later than he should have, the three of us decided. Once he did, his eyes were stung open, panicked and reddened. He looked as if he had descended more deeply into the underworld than he ever intended.

He gasped as if an invisible hand had been holding him down, breathless, while trying to make him face a world to which he had pledged indifference. He dog-paddled over to the side and dragged his belly like a pendulum across each ladder rung. The water was too cold, he insisted. He didn't see the point in this, and I laughed a little at his small anguish. Meanwhile we both were missing the beauty of the stalactites gripping the ceiling.

He hadn't necessarily wanted to come here, however. My mom had been the one who thought we needed contact with water flowing beneath the earth's surface. Only a few years before both my parents' cancer diagnoses, before my sister and I understood we were losing them forever, my mom was the one who wanted to begin helping her daughters find a source of life that transcended human bodies, transcended places. My dad for his part had complained repeatedly about the long lines for customs. He made it clear he would rather have stayed at home and rested. Maybe he had less of a sense, though, than his wife did that our home was only mud falling down a mountain, that everything was falling faster than any of us wanted.

The next day, we left our hotel in the early morning to climb a pyramid with moss blanketing its foundation. The structure had been built as a temple to a god the Mayans envisioned as a plumed serpent. During the vernal and autumnal equinoxes, the afternoon sun casts triangular shadows against the northwestern face of the pyramid, creating the illusion of the serpent god slinking down its steps. Our guide mentioned the pyramid's apex also served as a site for the sacrifice of young virgins, meant to coax the gods into providing a good harvest. As he said this, my dad only looked at me and nodded. Within our guide's hearing, he added everyone was guilty of some self-interest. He couldn't keep himself from observing aloud and too loudly that being from a primitive civilization alone, one with gods and goddesses, didn't mean you had more wisdom. If killing a virgin made your crops grow better after years of famine, he confessed he himself might be tempted.

My sister was the first to walk toward the pyramid and begin scaling steps whose edges were all smooth and rounded, while I stayed standing beside my parents. I was content to stay in the shade, fanning myself with my fingertips, doing nothing more than witnessing the other climbers' exertions. After a few minutes spent watching the crowds ascend the gleaming monolith in the near and treeless distance, my dad surprised me by walking toward it. I watched his bulk extend itself over the steps of an ancient ruin. At length, realizing I should also take advantage, I followed him.

Once we reached the pyramid's summit, my dad and I both were a little shaken by the fact there was no rope, no guard-rail at the precipice, which seemed to be crowded with too many other tourists. The stone forming the pyramid had grown smooth to silken from centuries of erosion. Beneath my tennis shoes, it felt rain slicked. My sister had reached the base again by the time my dad and I stood staring out onto the jungled vastness, afraid of the pyramid's slipperiness, not wanting to sacrifice ourselves for people whose gods had failed to save them. Now they were half history, half legend. All their dead virgins in the end made no difference.

Still for as long as they lived, there was a river flowing underneath them, always present. If the earth houses liquid intestines—if there are more underground rivers than anyone has yet discovered, as our guide mentioned once in passing—then these rivers also connect to an appendix. I say this only because more life always stirs inside any given person or ecosystem than ever becomes visible on the surface. Beneath the skin of every human body, the appendix attached to our own intestines serves as evidence of our ongoing evolution, proof no species can stay stagnant but must continue adapting to life's ceaseless need for movement. The fact we have evolved beyond a certain organ so it no longer fulfills a purpose signals only that nature intends us to keep living, even while life keeps inflicting a series of endings.

By the time we learned of the Mayans' ritual sacrifice of virgins, I was still years away from learning to feel the river running deep within my body, from needing this as solace. I hadn't known then that sensing this current was something that might soothe me amid so much absence, of my parents as well as the home and farm that went with them. Now I can lie down in the darkness during a power outage and feel a nameless river's presence while waiting for the mudslides to offer me salvation.

It was only after my sister had begun talking about visiting the cenote again on that Friday evening, only after her children had fallen asleep and I was trying and failing to do the same upstairs in the guest bed, that I realized I had been bathed briefly in transcendence, following my dad, mom, and sister off an outcropping of granite. Whatever else happened, we had been baptized in that sacred well together. My dad may have stayed underwater for ten seconds longer than he wanted. I may have surfaced too quickly to savor the feeling. Only now do I see clearly how I sculled much faster than was necessary over to the ladder to follow my family. I dried myself off a couple minutes before I needed.

MY NOSE was running when I returned to the city after my weekend in Indiana without electricity. My throat felt sore and scratchy. I felt the beginnings of the cold I had half expected to catch once the soap sat on the bathroom counter in my sister's home for two days dry and lifeless. A week later, and my voice was still weak, my eyes red and watery. Walking to buy myself medicine, I passed a man who more than likely sleeps in the homeless shelter only a couple blocks away from the apartment I share with my husband. Whenever he asks for money outside the pharmacy, his voice sounds low and melodic. Though the shelter must force him to leave its premises during the day, though his life lacks all security, he seems strangely contented in all weather, all seasons.

My voice was so ragged from coughing by then that I didn't bother responding when he asked me how I was doing. Instead, I walked past him, ignoring the unwanted attentions of a man whose clothes emit a sour odor, who often eyes me too closely from a couple blocks' distance. When I walked back inside my apartment, though, I acknowledged he has access to the same river as everyone else flowing through him. His life is no less real, no less valid. As I unwrapped another throat lozenge, I also wondered whether this man often seems to pay more attention to me than others walking past him because at some level he recognizes someone who maintains as little interest as he does in a world without permanence. Perhaps he understands my envy of pigeons, sea turtles, and salmon.

As MANY times as I have told myself the story of how the world ends, a rebirth likely happens just as often. Normally I tell myself this other story once I wake in the early mornings, when the world feels fresh again. From the mud that once washed away those who had forgotten they were nothing more than moving water themselves in essence, I imagine some crying erupts after a certain period. Silence transitions into a kind of music in what may or may not be a cyclical process. This crying announces the prelude to another civilization, one formed of thousands of babies who have been hatched of the earth's long quiet. Born of mud alone, having squeezed through the bodies of no women, their skin stays dirty until the rain falls down on their heads in a gentle effluence. These infants retain no memory of the race preceding them. This fresh crop of human beings turns their gazes toward the mountains, never conceiving that any mud could ever come to destroy them. They nourish no dreams of building any houses. In their innocence, they have no need of preserving what the rains would only wash away again.

For every early morning when I envision another species of humanity emerging in this dream of purity, by evening I cannot help foreseeing their disappearance. By the time the sun has vanished and I have lain down in my bed again, even a new race of human beings, one surviving on only wild grasses and the bark of trees, begins adhering to the same narrative as those who went before them. I have recently read that Charles Darwin once suggested the appendix aided in tree bark digestion, reminding us how our species used to live far more simply. But tree bark eventually becomes tasteless, especially to people destined to grow beyond the appendix's function while still carrying the weight of the past alive inside them. The children and grandchildren of those who once lived as purely as Adam and Eve inside their garden in time will build houses at the feet of mountains, forgetting their ancestors were born of mud alone, forgetting that everything must merge again into this same substance. Once the rains come unabated, another iteration of humanity finds itself lost, swallowed by a river's current.

OUR LAST day in Mexico, my parents wanted no more Mayan ruins. They wanted to enjoy the sun instead, to lie splayed like jellyfish on the sand outside our hotel lobby. Lying on a towel in between them, I felt slightly embarrassed at the wobbliness of their bodies as they adjusted themselves against their beach towels, spreading fat from their skeletons. An hour or so after our sunbathing started, I walked back inside our room, making some excuses so I could spend time alone in the air conditioning, reading in the shade of the curtains. When I stepped back onto the beach again, my mom introduced me to a man in his early twenties, maybe a couple years older than myself then. Improbably handsome with teeth whose whiteness matched the caps of the nearby waves, he was leaning back on his elbows, staring up into thin passing clouds, before he turned to talk to my mom and started laughing at something she said to him.

As he left us to take his surfboard into the water, my mom smiled and said my sister, now lying on her stomach with her bikini straps unknotted, had made friends with him. Glad I was wearing a one-piece, I felt some slight distaste for her comfort with her body in front of my parents. She has always been more at home in this world, though, than I have, and this was evidence. I have never asked her if she ever takes time to feel a river running through her circulatory system, throughout the full extension of her limbs, if she even finds this necessary. Her life is now so busy with her two young children, her days in southern Indiana so grounded, I tend to doubt it. Sometimes I forget how thoughts of the world's end, of a coming salvation, are only for those with the luxury of a warm apartment but who at times still feel homeless.

I can no longer remember if I went swimming that last afternoon in the Yucatán. Something tells me, though, I didn't. Knowing myself, it wouldn't surprise me if I spent the rest of the afternoon wishing I could swim once more in the cenote instead, missing the joy of the waves spread out before my feet in the process. I normally appreciate experiences more after they have already happened, though I remember my mom had been eager to take advantage of the splendor in the offing. The only person who had not climbed the pyramid was the first to wade into the turquoise expanses stretching out into the ocean. As her pale calves dissolved into the waves, her thigh backs were trembling.

I turned toward my dad to see if he was watching. I took off my sunglasses so he could see my eyes as I told him he should go and join her. But his blunt shoulder blades only wedged themselves more deeply into the fibers of his towel after I said this. His toenails seemed to arch and lengthen into a smooth sepulcher of sand. From the shoreline, my mom squealed, announcing the water was too cold for her to venture any farther. She shook her graying hair loose into the water's spray and trundled back smiling. Her knee cracked a little as she folded her body down beside me, as if truly tired from this exertion. My right knee now makes the same sound, assuming the end is near, whenever the time comes to bend.

45

WISDOM
TEETH

MAN IN THE MOON

I cannot look at his arms, his face. Because I want to lick the hair inside his navel, because I can never come close enough to see then straighten it with ribbons of saliva. Because the man in the moon isn't a man at all. He is only illusion known as pareidolia. The reason I cannot see his arms, his face, his knees is simple. He does not have them.

His nose, his jaw, his eyelashes are only patterns in stimuli science says are random. Astronomers affirm his facial features are basaltic formations born of volcanic eruptions. Their iron concentrations render them less reflective than the highlands. The man's eyes and mouth are no more than depressions compared with the higher plains surrounding them.

Yet you cannot confront a face, even one known as an illusion, without also seeing its expression. You cannot see the man in the moon without also perceiving a sadness embedded deep within his basaltic depressions. Still he never cries, because his world is waterless. Still early astronomers mistook the iron concentrations for oceans. Within his nostrils' nave, they saw dolphins.

Their term "lunar seas" persists as jargon among those who insist the moon is faceless, those who press telescopes to eyelids searching the craters' depressions until they've gone blind to the man in the moon's emotions. Likely the only advantage of loneliness is other worlds hold more promise. Anything shaped remotely like an almond becomes an eye to be seen with. Earlier astronomers and I have at least that much in common. We have both seen life on the moon that never existed.

They have all died, though, too early to know this. They have died and left me alone to see a face in the moon's oceans, a face that has become transparent, because water makes up most of any solid-looking body. In what were lakes or rivers to earlier astronomers, I see lips whose peaks crest the same as tidal waters being pulled by yet another moon's greater gravitation. Lips too cannot be random, and the man in the moon knows this. He knows his lips are no accident, if only because so long has passed with no one to touch them. Even a dentist brushing them in the course of an operation would now be welcome. A dentist extracting a tooth gone rotten.

Decades have elapsed since any astronauts have grazed his surface. His lips' dryness, the fact that none of the astronauts who have visited him have been women, should render me a good companion. He looks on always at our planet, his looking endless, at the same tilt of his head, a result of the moon and earth's synchronous orbit. The fact that I'm the only one who sees him I doubt he takes time to notice.

Other women, though, may have caught his interest. Other women may give him an erection as they undress by the light of his sun's reflection, while to astronomers seeing only basaltic formations, he vanishes. Perhaps to me alone he's indifferent. Perhaps the only reason he denies me his attention is because I've denied someone else before him. His amygdala alone eclipses constellations. His memory hovers colossal in the heavens.

I have more memories too than I know what to do with. When I was seven or eight, I was swinging on the set my dad had built from two fallen telephone poles he shortened. I was swinging and singing with the sun setting, a song that was less a song than my thoughts put to music. I was singing "I need a man, I need a man," over and over again to no real melody. I described this man I only imagined as smelling of soap, of having no hair in his armpits. But "I need a man, I need a man," I half sang, half spoke regardless when my dad surprised me. He was walking to our house from our garden and asked, "How about your daddy?"

He was only joking, was only being friendly. Still he had intruded, had done something invasive. I had gotten lost on purpose and he had found me. I thought I had a private life then at once knew I didn't. Years later, I never understood how other girls had boyfriends, how they sat at dinner with their fathers withstanding the knowledge they had been kissed or sexually excited. I had revealed the deepest part of me, the yearning that is there from almost the beginning. Ever afterward, I felt a little restricted in his company.

For me to be free, I would have to expose less of my longings. Because desire occupies vast spaces, I knew even then I would need a certain distance from my parents. I would need it then resent when they both grew sick just as I'd become a married woman. Reluctantly, I moved back with my young husband where I again could be seen too clearly.

Meanwhile, hunters walking through a black forest think a white fawn signals their death. They think she is an omen rather than something living, because she roams without any pigment. She roams deeper into the trees' darkness, imagining the moon alone as her natural companion. She imagines this because of his same whiteness. The imagining, though, does not bridge the distance, does not make her any less anomalous in a world more verdant.

The man in the moon sees the lost fawn and the whole world with it. He sees but does nothing, because he knows lostness resides within the lost object on such a small planet. He knows this and more from his higher vantage, from which he has also seen me packing more than a decade before this. From the skies, he has seen me leaving while remaining bound by gravity to the same surface. My mom had died already while my dad was scheduled for another round of chemotherapy. The man in the moon and I both watched, both of us healthy.

He must have seen me fold my bedding inside a suitcase through a cloud fallen over half his face. Once I decided I was going, was abandoning the only person left to whom I remained necessary, I told myself my dad didn't need me until I became convincing. I told myself this because I was living for the man in the moon already, for all the men who might be illusions—there are so many—you see walking through a city. With my dad still breathing, with my husband willing to indulge my whims, I began living for someone who exists only in theory.

I STILL live where there are more eyes to see and soon forget me, where I am lost amid so many faces wearing the same expression expressing nothing. This morning, I woke with my nose bruised and swollen, with no one noticing the difference the day's remainder except for my husband. The bruise appeared after I walked into a glass wall last evening. Someone had washed the wall transparent. I walked into what looked to be an open door to the restaurant where we were eating but whose food I didn't finish.

A friend has just reminded me we are meeting for dinner this evening. I cannot go, I've decided, because I look too ugly. The man in the moon, though, may care less about appearances if no more astronauts visit him within another decade. Eventually, he might look past me leaving my dad too early, the loss of whom has since carved hollow spaces within me, arid depressions earlier astronomers might have mistaken for seas. The absence has eroded mountains into valleys where my nose and eyes should be. The craters, I mean.

This is the third time I've walked into a wall of glass, allowing light through but not me with it. The problem isn't my prescription, because I have gotten new glasses. An optometrist can correct your vision but not decide where you fix your attention. And I am always looking into the distance. Your eyes forget to focus, insists my husband. Watch where you're walking, he cautions. Look at the glass rather than through it, because next time you may do real damage. This notch on your nose as it is may be permanent.

What are you seeing instead of the glass? my husband might wonder but doesn't bother asking. The question also might not occur to him because in the man in the moon he has no interest. Because he thinks his love for me sufficient. Because of leaving my dad stranded he has almost forgotten but I haven't. Because his absence hasn't carved hollow, unreflective places within him some might perceive as faces. Because he is so much more solid a person while I feel half a ghost as it is, someone who should walk through glass without pain, without bruising, but cannot manage.

BEFORE HIS hospice started, a nurse visited him once a week in the home where he had recently begun living alone. She cleaned the port on his arm he never had removed for chemo's poison. She checked his blood pressure and felt his head for its temperature, as if nothing more were wrong with him than a fever. She asked about his bowel movements once when I walked into the kitchen and they were one room over. My dad joked she needed to know everything.

When she left, my dad said she was attractive. In truth, she was overweight and her hair dyed too dark for her complexion. But my dad had needed to find her pleasing, and I saw this. With my mom two months buried, he was lonely and looking. He was unembarrassed by his desire even as he himself was dying. Empty as the house was without my mom's presence, it began filling with his need. It made the room the nurse left crowded in her absence.

IN WHAT looks each night the same to me when the moon makes an appearance, different cultures see different images. The only consensus about the man most agree to be human is that he is being punished for some transgression. Medieval Christian tradition claims he is Cain barred from heaven. Old Germanic cultures imagined he'd stolen his neighbor's garden hedge.

Roman lore says he stole a sheep, a larger crime in ancient civilization. Whereas Chinese mythology maintains the man is a goddess, banished from earth after consuming a potion meant to ensure her life was endless. The Chinese have also spotted moon rabbits, while many London taverns during the Middle Ages named themselves the "Man in the Moone" as a way of boosting business. Bartenders claimed he spent his days drinking claret as evidence. Sober or drunken, the fact remains he lives in permanent isolation.

It's all over now, I still want to tell him. Hardly anyone these days drinks claret. No one believes there ever was a Cain much less a heaven from which he was denied entrance. I am the only person left who thinks you exist to begin with. I have nearly broken my nose in search of someone who may be either an illusion or a rabbit, someone whose theft or murder or alcoholism is never forgiven. A woman who made herself fatherless a few months before she needed.

THE ONLY time my dad ever hit me was after I'd gone missing, in SeaWorld of all places. Hours passed with my parents looking for me. I imagine we all were hungry then. When they came to the information booth where a man had brought me once he found me crying, my mom was relieved and hugged me. My dad guessed correctly I'd gotten lost on purpose. He said I'd done it for attention. In front of the information booth's attendant, he bent me over and spanked me.

It happened only once but was still a violation, less of my body than of my thinking. He had seen through me as if my head were made of glass while my mom saw nothing. He had known

I'd grown sick of my parents paying more attention to my younger sibling than to myself and the dolphins. The show itself they hardly noticed in their love of someone so small as to make little difference. I didn't follow them when the show was finished. Had they only turned around to look for me, they never would have lost me. I had not gone missing but stood there stationary.

And this lost fawn in the forest. I sometimes suspect she has no one except a pareidolic illusion as a companion because this is how she likes it. Because there are other fawns in the forest, and she could find them if she wanted. None may have her same whiteness. None may reflect the moon with her same precision, but still they speak the same language. Still they might discuss matters affecting the larger deer population.

Only in their concerns regarding the state of the forest, in their dialectical considerations, she takes no interest. She prefers the man in the moon's lips, which are gray and chipped, which are large enough to swallow her whole. She could find herself, she thinks, in his digestive system. Falling down his esophagus, she could make sense of all this lostness once she is chewed to pieces. Her blankness then would serve a purpose other than hastening hunters to an early death because of their own superstitions. She would become food to keep the man alive with.

The man in the moon, however, is only a fragment. Even if his mouth exists, he likely has no stomach, no intestines. He suffers from severe limitations, if only because another planet once collided with our own according to geologists, creating the moon amid solar torrents. The moon consists of the earth's own crust and mantle as evidence. Still the man in the moon must have teeth to chew his food with. The white fawn thinks this with such seriousness she thinks she knows this, though in truth she only guesses. Given enough time, the man in the moon might visit the dentist.

As a person with only a head, he also has his opinions. He must have after witnessing so much of our destruction, more than he likely wishes. He may suppose we too are only phantoms, nothing more than his brain's hallucinations. And he may be correct, though no one asks him. He may be a god or godless. He may be speaking as we gaze through our windows up toward his depressions. He may be, though we cannot hear him.

The bruises on my nose have darkened to the color of lunar seas. They have blackened into what may become iron concentrations, providing me with some small consolation. With his eyes focused on my lowlands, the man in the moon can perhaps now see me better from a distance. I leave him to his own conclusion about what data are random.

Will I ever even meet him? No, the answer is obvious. I know nothing more of him than astronomers for certain. But love fills in spaces. Love heightens your attention. Love of a man not on the moon but in it, a man so deeply embedded within its rock he can never flee its surface. A man lighter than I am owing to the moon's lower gravitation. A man not emitting light but lightness.

Before unpacking all my boxes in my new apartment, I came home again at the doctor's insistence. My dad needed someone to care for him, to keep him from getting cuts or bruises, because the chemo made him highly susceptible to infection. The doctor called me and said two weeks at minimum. Though I ended up staying longer, my dad and I agreed one week was sufficient.

The first day with me home to watch him, he wanted to install new window screens to save money on air conditioning. I told him I would do it, but he said that if this was his life now, it wasn't worth it. This new life of constant exhaustion. This being bedridden with the windows closed to the birds that flew into them. A nick from the window's edge I knew could kill him, but I didn't try to stop him. I agreed the house needed better air circulation.

He would also save some birds in the process, one human life on its tail end for that of a few feathered friends. Because this always happened. All throughout the summer, birds flew into our living room windows and died from internal bleeding, from hemorrhages to the brain and hidden bruises. Afterward, we swept them from the porch into a wheelbarrow we emptied in our garden. They flew too quickly against what looked transparent but was as close as something can come to solid. Sometimes we laughed at their carcasses, at their thinking we lived in a house with no windows for protection, but where they were flying we could never ask them.

That they were trying to reach the moon now seems apparent. Anyone who has seen a bird's silhouette thrown against the moon's stark brightness knows this. Anyone who has ever tried to follow birds flying past one cloud to another hanging yet higher in the firmament realizes how hopeless they must find reaching their destination. Still they flap and fly to exhaustion as the moon's attraction weakens their resistance. Then if you have wings and the moon looks within access, the man's hollow spaces a viable place to rest, you use them.

And this same lost fawn in the forest. She has lost herself for only one reason, to claim all the moon's attention. She has gotten lost solely to seek what he still refuses. He comes no closer when she begs him, so all she can do is wait for her first menstruation, when all the world's female mammals shed their uterine lining in league with the moon's wholeness. She can wait to see if this brings her any closer to him. She can wait and be disappointed. She can live all her life devising yet another stratagem.

I TOOK advantage of being home again to have my wisdom teeth removed by my childhood dentist. While my dad's white blood cell shortage kept him weak and struggling for oxygen, I underwent sedation. The dentist brushed my lips with tissue every few minutes. He wiped away blood leaching from my gums in what seemed a soothing rhythm. After he had numbed their pinkness, the feeling in my lips intensified as if to strike a balance. Their nerves began tingling, and each gentle wipe of tissue felt a small gift. Almost too soon, the operation ended.

For the pain to come once the anesthetic receded, he prescribed me Vicodin. Yet instead of the euphoria promised, I grew nauseous. The whole night I vomited. I read my dad's concern in his expression when I padded to the bathroom between our bedrooms in the morning again. He had no energy, though, to speak as he lay on his deathbed, as I nursed my mouth with aspirin. What was meant to be a brief convalescence became the beginning of his hospice. After another hospital visit, the doctor confirmed he was too weak to withstand the bone marrow transplant that had been promised. The chemotherapy that had previously proved effective his body now rejected.

And in this a lightness. A weightlessness I have not felt since. Inside me, air briefly replaced something solid. The end was almost completed, something fragrant exchanged for something rotted. Because when everything collapses, something else arises. An emptiness that is also freedom, the mouth released from its hard, yellow teeth of wisdom. Because every life is in some sense a prison. This world is only so large a one to get lost in.

Hearing the final diagnosis, something in me lifted the same as a flying fish breaching the waves of the ocean, one whose pelvic fins have evolved solely for beating the air above water's surface for hundreds of feet in the distance. Like moths, flying fish are attracted by luminescence. Nights when the moon is clouded, night fishermen await them with electric light filling their canoes, exploiting this instinct. And this love of a man in the moon—perhaps not even a person—may also have his henchmen. They may be the ones making glass walls look like doors just opened.

I still cannot fully explain this sense of liberation, this looking toward the moon, as I realized then my dad was dying for certain, as if all I had ever wanted was his absence. Because of all people living, my dad was the only one to know me wholly, to read every thought I ever had without me voicing it. Without him, I have lost the world's recognition. Without him, my world is too private. Without him, I am a lost white fawn in the forest. No one now sees my same features reflected in his own. Even were he beside me at this moment, my nose is no longer a replica of his, small and bulbous. Instead, it has grown wide and blue and swollen. Its new notch may be permanent.

AFTER THE mortician came to dress my dad's body, after he'd lain for eight or more hours dead in his pajamas, his body stiffened as expected. Yet his lips whose shape I have inherited fell slack, his face revealing no new expression.

My sister was the first to notice. Once the gurney was unloaded from the van, his lips turned up slightly at the edges. Minutes later, we both saw the smile widen. His teeth began showing through lips that parted then stretched themselves into something radiant. Together we stood and watched it happen. By the time the mortician wheeled him past the window the birds flew to their death against, he too was laughing at the transformation. At this small, soft planet careened out of orbit. At the gap between his two front teeth that is mine as well. These series of spaces visible only when we feel a sense of lightness.

And this white fawn, this white fawn again. She chews only low, jaundiced grasses, because winter has returned to the forest. No acorns, no apples and persimmons, because this world has turned colorless. She should feel at home here now as a consequence, but she doesn't. A person running through the snow-covered forest could run into her and hurt himself if he ran fast enough. Fortunately, everyone keeps their distance.

There is no reason to have your wisdom teeth removed if chewing causes no discomfort or pain. Still my dentist recommended it once I left my dad at home to ask him, because these teeth are more susceptible to cavities, to gaping holes within, because their position makes them harder to access for cleaning. Since my parents received their separate cancer diagnoses, I'd had eight cavities filled over two appointments. I asked and paid for gas at each because of the extent of the damage, because of all the hard matter inside me gone missing.

And it isn't love I mean. It isn't that at all. The love has stayed. What has gone is wisdom only. What has gone is knowing anything as definite. What has replaced it may be all illusion. I no longer need a man, only an empty planet. A place of yet greater freedom now that once sprung from my dad's absence has vanished.

I'VE RECENTLY read about a woman who tried to teach a dolphin English. She painted her lips black, the rest of her face whitened, so the dolphin could better read their movements. The study took place in the Virgin Islands and received funding from NASA. This happened not long after the man in the moon spent time with Neil Armstrong and Buzz Aldrin, because teach dolphins our language and we might teach aliens, or so went the 1960s logic. The woman slept suspended in a bed above the dolphin. At night, she encircled it with a shower curtain.

The man leading the study injected the dolphin with psychotropics to speed the animal's development, a fact later making the study infamous. More interesting to me, however, is the fact the dolphin fell in love with the woman. The rubbing he did with his erections left her legs with bruises.

He also ran his teeth up and down her legs in courtship, something that may and may not be particular to love between dolphins and humans. Teeth are precious regardless of the fact I kiss only with my lips, keeping my teeth hidden, regardless of the fact I have paid to have a dentist remove those with any wisdom. Then again there is something to eating and being eaten. This the woman, though, avoided. Astronauts traveling to the moon have also escaped the consequences of landing in the man's largest orifice, of falling prey to hunger without any means of digestion.

When I walked into the glass wall last evening at the restaurant's entrance, my nose absorbed all the damage, protecting my teeth in the process. Perhaps because the man in the moon's nose sits lower than its surrounding highlands, he is toothless. Perhaps Neil Armstrong and Buzz Aldrin were free to land anywhere they wanted because all his teeth have been hit by falling comets. His nose that is no nose at all has failed to shield them. The galaxy's debris have eroded all his wisdom, making a dentist redundant.

My dad paid for me to have braces, to remove the gap between my two front teeth I inherited from him, because he said teeth were what really made a woman attractive, because he said he wished his parents had done the same for him. The gap, though, has partially returned and persisted, a gap that makes me lisp and spit when I speak too quickly. My dad tried to make me pretty, but instead I spray saliva into people's faces while trying to communicate too much in earnest.

In her diary, the woman who tried to teach the dolphin English but never succeeded recorded her fear of being harmed, of being broken. To allay the dolphin's affection, she eventually gave him hand jobs on a daily basis. Yet once NASA stopped funding the project, the dolphin stopped breathing. He committed suicide once she left him to go get married. Love, though, does these things. Love frees itself from bodies. Even my dad's corpse knew this. It said so without saying anything, only smiling.

LAST NIGHT I lay on our bed looking at all the other apartments separated from ours by a slim strip of cement. Only from this angle can I ever see the man embedded in the moon's depressions for some past transgression. Last night, though, the sky was clouded. Instead of reading or watching TV while my husband worked late, I turned off all our lights and watched a man whose blinds were half open.

I lay down on the bed in the darkness and watched him fold shirts inside a suitcase. I lay on my side without moving, wondering where he was going. I imagined from the suit jackets he took from their hangers after the shirts were folded that he was traveling somewhere on business, to another city likely much like the one he was leaving. For the moment, though, I pretended he was taking an airplane into a forest, that he would find the lost white fawn if the moon wouldn't.

And he must have seen me looking. He must have felt my eyes more than seen them across the cement, because there was no moon to shed any light into my apartment. He was in any case leaving me stranded. He was leaving and I had nearly fallen asleep when I became aware of his absence. I covered myself with a blanket and left my own blinds open. When my husband came home, he shut them.

Water cannot survive on the moon's surface owing to low atmospheric pressure. Yet water molecules hover in the atmosphere's thin layer of gases. Some astronomers still posit lunar seas may have existed for this reason; in time, the seas may have only evaporated. In the moon's eyes and nose may once have swum dolphins looking down with love on humans. The male dolphins may have gotten erections from those undressing with their blinds open, while the little white fawn is willing herself to stop breathing but has not succeeded.

COCCYX

THE MERMAIDS OF AUSTIN

During the early 1960s, more than ten thousand children were born with arms so small they resembled fins of flesh. Their legs too were unnaturally shortened. Only half survived their infancy, and those who did were termed teratogenic, or "monster forming," a word reflecting how these newborns must initially have struck their parents. While still floating inside amniotic fluid, their bodies had contracted into a shape better suited for a world made of water alone, for a life spent among mermaids and mermen. If they had only been allowed to swim throughout their lifetimes rather than being forced to negotiate sidewalks and indoor flooring, they may ultimately have been better adapted for a world with a warming climate, a world that now seems to be returning to one of mostly water with the rising oceans. If their stunted limbs only meant other processes too had been stunted—if these children only kept rather than lost the tail that grows in utero from each human coccyx before falling away as an atavistic remnant—they might have emerged as a new iteration of our species, if one also evoking creatures of legend. As it is, doctors later determined this string of birth defects resulted from a drug known as thalidomide, widely prescribed at the time for morning sickness. In addition to undeveloped limbs, unintended consequences to the fetus included a high incidence of blindness and deafness. That the only man affected by this condition I have ever met is also immune to electric charges is only coincidence.

I sat beside him on stage at the Museum of the Weird, a modern curiosity cabinet, not long after my husband and I had finished eating Easter breakfast down in Austin. Chosen as his assistant, I sat swinging my legs while facing several families with young children who were waiting for a man born a merman to close his lips over wires live with electric current. Before performing this feat, he explained that no one else should attempt to do the same under any circumstances. If any of us made similar gambits, we would die of the experience. As he spoke, I watched his small arms gesture with the flourish and extravagance of a lifelong showman.

A couple minutes before I found myself on stage beside him, my gaze had fixed itself on what a nearby plaque claimed to be a yeti skeleton. I had looked away on purpose when he asked for a volunteer from the audience. A boy behind me raised his arm as he panted, desperate to be chosen. But I had worn a dress the color of seafoam and cut low in the bodice, a dress fanning out from my waist with the longing of a thousand river deltas emptying themselves into the ocean. I had also bought shoes the color of sand to match it, and the showman was a merman, one who likely missed the nearness of the sea while living in Austin. He had no choice except to pick the woman dressed like a mermaid, he explained to the boy's parents. This man whose arms mimicked the fins of something more aquatic than human must have imagined me still with the tail once fallen from my coccyx, one that in another lifetime would have enabled swifter underwater movement.

THE DAY before this, my husband and I had been walking near some street musicians, when he lingered to hear another song and I walked ahead, browsing Day of the Dead skeletons filling a shop window. A policeman pulled up and stopped his car beside me. Leaning toward me while unrolling his window, he asked if I was working the district. I bent over and squinted into his sunglasses, trying to read his expression. Seeing nothing beyond my own reflection, I told him I was here only for the weekend. He nodded in a private silence as I walked on, absorbing his implication. He said no more to me, I imagine, because I looked better from a distance. Because I was once a mermaid, he a merman, though he had long forgotten our origins.

I was wearing a skirt I've had since college. I've grown no taller since I bought it, though in recent years it had seemed to shorten. My husband occasionally remarked on its dearth of fabric. Pleated faux leather, it suggested I may have once been a cheerleader when I have always been the opposite. We had come to Austin, though, because of the warmer climate along with the pleasure of exploring a new city in the early spring, when Chicago still evinces traces of winter. We had come for the sun and city's claim to weirdness, for the spectacle of witnessing the country's largest urban bat colony fly out to feed at sunset along with the food trucks, the musicians. The skirt had seemed appropriate when packing my bag back inside our apartment, but after being stopped by the policeman, my husband confirmed my suspicion when I asked him whether I looked like a sex worker wearing it, even if my legs are pale and scar-ridden, even if I'm no longer a young woman.

I kept walking until I reached an antique outlet, whose window ledges were littered with more human skulls painted white, many with flowers and spider webs drawn across their foreheads. I noticed the female skeletons all had scarves wrapped around their faces. All of these dead women, whose sex was signaled by their longer eyelashes and lipstick, preserved their modesty, while the male skeletons bared their teeth, happily naked. Though the weather here was warmer than predicted, I realized the scarves may have done more than shield the females from too much male attention. The women also must have wanted to disguise their ugliness. The scarves looking prettier than those behind them hid them from the intrusion of male gazes, from dismissal and assessment.

But my skirt would have to go. This was now decided. Once the skirt was gone, other things would have to go with it. First the skirt and then my legs hanging beneath too little fabric. Afterward, my feet would go and with them the toenails I had painted the cobalt of the cloudless sky blanketing all of Austin. This would be only the beginning of a lifelong process, one of returning to rather than evolving away from my origins, one that meant moving away from beauty and toward something closer to monster forming, closer to prehuman. Because you cannot slowly begin resembling a mermaid again—transforming back into a finned and primordial woman—without losing all that once filled your closet, everything you once thought you needed. Whenever I take time now to think of Eve and Adam, I no longer believe Eden was a garden. The paradise we were once cast out of as a species must have been an ocean instead. Of this I feel certain, if only because all life evolved from the sea, including humans.

Later, near sunset, my husband and I stood on Congress Avenue Bridge waiting to watch nearly one and a half million bats emerge from beneath where we were standing. Facing the opposite of where the larger crowds gathered, I had convinced my husband to join me in avoiding the crush of so many onlookers. I still felt more exposed than I wanted while wearing the skirt I've had since college. Whenever too many people gather too closely together, my lifelong tendency has also always been to establish distance, and my husband has known me long enough to indulge me in silence. I told him some of the bats were sure to fly against the current, though in retrospect I doubt either of us believed this would happen. Potbellied men drinking tallboys and pedaling paddleboats with the plastic head of a swan between them had gathered on one side of the bridge alone, which told us all we needed. They spat into the ripples of Lady Bird Lake and waved up at the hundreds of other tourists.

A man wearing a stuffed bat glued to his baseball cap tapped me on my shoulder just as I acknowledged we would need to cross the bridge in order to witness the bulk of what his hat represented. He pulled his earlobes down toward his chin, signaling his deafness, before I had a chance to speak to him as he ushered us from one side of the bridge to the other, more concerned than we were that we would miss the diurnal migration. Given the hat he was wearing and his easy authority, I assumed he must have worked for the city, helping tourists like ourselves enjoy an optimal experience. He may have given tours in sign language or, if not, then identified with another species more than his own in some ways despite bats' exceptional hearing. Or perhaps his awareness of the disparity, knowing bats heard not only more than himself but beyond any human capacity, was what invited his awe and an emotional investment beyond my understanding. With his arms flying in any case toward the other side of the water, he urged us to hurry. He forced me into the throng, into the welter of my fellow species.

"All of the free-tailed bats roosting below us are female," a woman wearing heavy eyeliner and nearly as dark of lipstick offered to the crowd at large, to no one in particular. I folded my arms over the steel bannister and, because no one else responded, smiled as if she had answered a question I asked her. Half the crowd was wearing wind breakers. Their hoods were beating the air senseless, bruising ashen clouds and imprinting them with violet blotches as the woman with the eyeliner cleared her throat and emphasized a second time the fact these flying mammals were all women. They too had once crawled out from the sea, she didn't bother adding, however. She neglected to say they had eventually grown wings in the course of evolution to recover their freedom. Their furry tails, once fins, remained with them for balance. All these bats, unlike those awaiting their appearance, had retained what had grown from their coccyx. Within another few minutes they would emerge in flight, broaching transcendence.

I strained my eyes to glimpse a few bats flying out to forage earlier than the rest. I watched four or five circle a copse of fruit trees overspreading a stretch of parkland, where they stabbed at pendant figs and peaches. Their wings were splayed into webbed fingers looking almost human. A couple minutes later once the remaining bats awakened, they flew out almost as a single body, too fast for me to distinguish whether bats sink or swim once their wings eventually fail them, once they fall toward the water in exhaustion and at last are forced into confronting all the hidden life stirring beneath its surface. Their flight was too furious for me to decipher whether any descended back into the same warm cytoplasm where all life on earth began, where these female bats too in time might become different kinds of women.

As the last left the bridge's underbelly, I imagined mermaids were also leaving their mermen. All the mermaids of Austin were now sculling up from Lady Bird Lake's bottom as the stuffed bat of the deaf man came unglued from his cap and I watched him put it back inside his pocket. The mermaids were clambering onto rocks bordering new condominium developments. They clambered and then they rested, surveying this world's wreckage. They adjusted the holsters squeezing the scales of their hips, because even mermaids carry guns down in Texas. Soon they started firing their pistols at random as they watched the little-legged men scatter on the downtown streets of Austin. They laughed as they clapped their seashells together. Meanwhile the bats kept flying farther in the distance as their tails flapped behind them.

Walking back to our hotel room, my husband and I passed a miniature golf course filled with young families. I pointed toward an enormous statue of Peter Pan flanking the entrance when my husband ran and stepped between his legs. He grazed Peter where his penis should have been and wasn't, and I followed him through the gate. I followed with reluctance, because some of the children were screaming and throwing their golf clubs in a tantrum. As my husband took out his wallet, I confessed I didn't feel like playing. Not in a place with so many children when their world has been ravaged, when all too soon they will have to stop playing miniature golf to dissolve back into a warmer cytoplasm. Not when we have all discarded our scales and fins in the course of evolution for what seems little reason. Not when the collision of species is coming and promises to be orgiastic. All too soon and all too quickly, we will return to sameness, until there is no distinguishing a bat from a fish from a man or woman. My tail will then regrow itself from my coccyx, replicating the process once carried out inside my mother's body, before I remembered while swimming in fetal fluid that all the world has not yet become an ocean.

THE MAN whose performance figured as the main attraction inside Austin's Museum of the Weird on Easter morning seemed to harbor almost as much interest as we did in the holiday, which my husband and I have never celebrated apart from a large breakfast. Though when stepping inside the museum we had no idea this man with arms falling well above his waist existed, he also seemed to confirm our instincts for coming here to Austin. By this point in our weekend, we felt we had largely seen the city until we walked past this entrance, until we felt drawn by the prospect of carnival side shows, of grotesque anomalies. Inside the museum, the man who had once been poisoned inside his mother's womb struck me as an embodiment of my own private feelings of atrophying in a world and on a holiday made for people who still believed in spring's renewal, who still derived satisfaction from painted pastel eggs and plush rabbits. People who did not believe the end of the world was coming. People who had no conception the end comes by degrees rather than through cataclysm, with each accumulating inch of the rising oceans.

Whereas this man looked as if he were in the process of shedding needless length and needless appendages, preparing for a new stage in evolution. Because even as a grown man his body seemed unfinished, because I will likely die feeling the same despite having been spared thalidomide poisoning, I felt at home in his presence. I felt refreshed while watching him gesture solely from his wrists since his arms were elbowless. He wore a sleeveless undershirt and black pants rolled up at their edges. His long and curling hair, still auburn in his later fifties, fell past his shoulders. Before I sat in the audience for his performance, he looked a raw seafaring man from a distance. Up close, however, he looked even smaller than when my husband and I first approached the stage he dominated. His face was sunburned, weather beaten. Of everyone else in the audience, I alone can attest nothing ever shocked him. Inside his mouth, forks of electricity audibly crepitated, though he managed to swallow his bouquet of live wires without a problem.

He explained that as a child he had been struck by lightning, though nothing else happened. With the bravura of an actor who plays only one role throughout his lifetime, he claimed—almost boasted—there had been no damage. At the time, wanting nothing more than entertainment, I took what he said for granted without stopping to wonder whether he might have cultivated his immunity as a way of earning money through these performances, whether he had lived a life less straightforward than the story he presented. He declared nevertheless that a hair dryer dropped in the bathtub while plugged in could not affect him as he lathered, and I laughed along with the rest of the audience. This gift was unrelated, he added, to his other aberrations. Then following his instructions, I held a lightbulb to his skin after he sucked on the wires for several seconds. Raging with electric current, his body transformed the lightless bulb into a blistering brightness. Staring at his face, I was almost blinded. Sensing he must have been suffering and trying to hide it, looking out on all the other spectators instead, I found my gaping husband. I concentrated for a moment on someone who enjoyed the luxury of a body with normal proportions, someone a head taller than me and who could easily be electrocuted.

The man asked me to do this over and over again, touching the end of the lightbulb to his upper arm so everyone could watch it brighten. For the benefit of those filming us from their seats, I touched my fingers to his arm shaped like a fin and sparks flew between us, a mermaid and merman, the last of their species until life underwater once more becomes our only option. Toward the end of the performance, he asked me to fist bump his tiny hand, and a blue charge ricocheted between us. The sound reverberated throughout my own body—later my husband told me he could hear it. The man then asked everyone to clap for me, his mermaid assistant.

While walking toward the exit and leaving the man who made the museum most of its money to shock another audience, we confronted the corpse of a mermaid standing in the hallway. Kept behind a glass prison, what remained of her hinted she too was smaller than average. My husband laughed as my jaw fell open, as I read on a plaque that those mermaids taken from the Fiji Islands by Western charlatans like P.T. Barnum were originally crafted from monkey corpses. Villagers grafted the tails of fish onto their abdomens. Sometimes they glued extra scales on for embellishment. Only before Barnum got hold of his—before he exhibited it across the United States and Europe—poor South Pacific fishermen regarded them as totems, as emblems of something holy and pre-human. As something sacred. They neglected to design their mermaids as beautiful objects on purpose, because fall too in love with a body, as the fishermen intuitively understood, and you fail to accept that body changing, fail to see beyond its surface. Half fish and half mammalian, these mermaids that once horrified Barnum's public originally were intended to suggest a reality transcending what it means to be merely an animal, merely flesh overlaid on a skeleton.

The Western audience that paid to see Barnum's shows and exhibits knew no more of the Fiji mermaid's origins, however, than pregnant women in the 1960s did of a certain drug's consequences for their unborn children. In his autobiography, Barnum himself described his mermaid as "an ugly, dried-up, black-looking, and diminutive specimen. . . . its arms thrown up, giving it the appearance of having died in great agony." Yet in any circus or museum, mermaids are only worth the fee for admission if you wish at some level to be frightened, reminded of something you have always known inside your bloodstream but have kept quiet and hidden. In the Fiji mermaid in Austin, I felt I recognized the woman I was becoming. The mermaid who was once a monkey and I were both easily mistaken for other women. We were both uglier up close than expected. We both were in the process of surrendering to the course of evolution, both preparing to be submerged beneath an expanding ocean. Her mouth, even now, was wired permanently open. She looked, in death, as if she were still screaming from the hell she lived in, a carnival creature by virtue only of her isolation, her distance from the lushness of the Fiji Islands. However distasteful to the public, to me she remained holy, symbolic of all our destinies. A way forward that will allow us to return to our beginnings.

As my husband walked ahead of me out onto Sixth Street, I thought I heard her scream that beneath the sea she is only one of millions. Wearing my dress that conjured the color of coastal waters, I turned around, and she told me how she and other mermaids sleep all day along with the bats hanging beneath the bridge above them. Both are nocturnal species, both with exceptional hearing. Last evening, she had heard the woman in the crowd announce that all the foraging bats were women. She heard, and she understood the reason. Only once her fellow mermaids wake with the sun setting as the female bats are flying out to feast upon the city's insects—once they swim up toward the surface and see men staring at them as if they were hardly real and hardly living—do they pull their guns from their holsters. They protect their territory. They grow shameless.

PINKY
TOES

GHOST FEET

Not long after the house across the road was demolished, my parents pulled me outside to watch Halley's Comet drift past our barn, our grain bins. I'd be in my eighties—an old woman, my dad said—the next time I'd have a chance to see it. A light flying alone in the darkness. That was all the comet was to me in 1986. Were it anything besides what astronomers say it is—a ball of ice and dust, a remnant of the formation of other stars and planets—the comet would be me, untethered to this world, this body. Something in which I may have had more of an interest.

Standing in our yard, beneath the magnolia tree where grass had trouble growing, I dug my toes deeper into patches of dirt. I have no memory of seeing the comet, only of standing there restless, waiting to go back inside again. I never ran to try to keep pace with its tail as part of me imagines my parents may have wanted, performing the wonder that belonged to them instead. I

77

was seven years old and humoring them. My toes dirtied themselves, fidgeted. For what seemed like some time, I had already been deeply certain other worlds lay beyond this. I was also aware I had access to only my own, to only one of them. The comet proved nothing, did nothing to bridge the distance.

Shifting my weight, I watched the whites of my parents' eyes glint. A mist was falling inside them, shooting sparks off their eyelashes, slim swords of iridescence that quickly evaporated. A gentle rain was washing their skin from within. They clasped hands and stretched their necks up toward a sky enfolding our farm in an indigo blanket as the earth dampened my feet, blackening their bottoms. Looking back, I can see I missed the comet for their faces, shining with an ease of never knowing all that mattered, of never seeing all the beauty burning beyond them. A quality I still consider their shared essence.

The house across the road—razed into a heap of siding a couple weeks before we saw the comet—lay half a mile away at the end of another driveway overgrown with tawny grasses. From our front porch swing, it stood visibly collapsing, an island of dusk and shadow spaces. No larger than my fingertip from that vantage, I could pierce it with my fingernail, toppling it if I wanted. Whenever I was tempted, I put my hand back in my lap, though, resisting. Were anyone living there, they would have been our closest neighbors. Maybe even friends. As it was, the house only reminded me we didn't have any. After the corn and soybeans were harvested in autumn, the fields sat empty. Few trees were left growing at their edges. Most farmers preferred to cut them down as saplings for easier mowing.

I was left alone enough that I could walk there often, no one asking where I was going, no one pausing to worry about the splintering floorboards or rats burrowing beneath them, the fallen shingles or lopsided ceiling. Born amid wide, open spaces, I longed for walls, enclosure from what now feels like the beginning. I stuck a couple crayons in my pocket to color in pages of black-and-white drawings of unicorns scaling mountains, of octopuses splaying

padded their nests with swatches of flannel shirts, cotton dresses. A girl my same age in the family may have lived here with less love too than she once wanted. In the end, it made no difference. She left while her shoes stayed. Now only ghost feet filled them.

Sometimes the farmer who owned the field on whose far corner the house stood slanting and somnolent drove his pickup through the tawny grasses to ask me what I was doing. I can no longer remember what I told him, only that the back of his neck, crosshatched with decades of living bared to the elements, startled me when he turned his head toward a flock of starlings or tractor groaning in the distance. I must have been too young for him to have suspected me of vandalism. Fear of the house harming me or someone like me was likely part of the reason he soon rid his acreage of what remained of its shingles and siding. After the house as good as evaporated, I knew I should have taken some shoes home with me before they were buried. I should have made a quiet corner for them in my closet. In all the time I spent there, I never tried on a pair. I never found out if any of them fit me.

Going unnoticed by someone who sat beside me throughout the school day perhaps should have left me less wounded than it did. The fact I allowed this early taste of love's absence to inflict real damage likely only speaks to everything else I was given, all the love and warmth of my parents, all the freedom of empty spaces flanked by long grasses. Still the daily portions of non-love that came from a boy whose eyes were blue to blazing reinforced a separation I felt already, from having no one except my sister near me to play with, from having difficulty making friends when placed among those who were also seven.

From all the time I spent alone coloring on the steps of a house long abandoned, I still believe I came closer to acceptance. I went to school next morning then returned home again haunted by a face I saw directly only when he needed to borrow paper or pencils. I realized you can spend your evenings haunted by as many phantasms as you wish, but this changes nothing in the world outside your eyelids. Had something brighter than a comet not held me captive so early, I might not have associated swarms of indifferent faces with real living. I might not have stayed so long in the same city where seas of them fill all the open spaces.

After the house across the road was demolished, I didn't miss it. Watching rats scurry deeper into hiding when I walked along floorboards splintering more each time I went was never pleasant. I felt some small relief when I could simply stay in my yard and swing or chase my dog instead. Next year at school, I sat beside someone different. I also fell a little in love with him, this time without any hurt from no love flowing back in my direction. I knew now not to expect it, though secretly I hoped I had some pure, some flaming essence, which might become visible once enough time elapsed. I developed some of the arrogance of a comet, something my parents regarded as clean, as resplendent, because of only distance, because no one on earth could touch it. I hoped there was some starlight lurking beneath a face and body too ordinary to be noticed. Later, more pain came from doubting anything good ever came of all my isolation.

At age ten or eleven, I learned in one of my classes how gravity is nothing more than a large object warping space's fabric. Our teacher said the sun sinks inside its weave the same as an apple does a flimsy basket. Both comets and planets slip inside the grooves forming around this star at the center of our solar system and in so doing assume an orbit. Even the heavens, in other words, undergo warping and depression. Even the heavens are easily wrinkled, dented. They are forever changed by something rolling thoughtlessly over top of them. After I moved away from wide, open spaces and accepted some small love from boys, from men, I felt unoriginal, common. My body's responses to their touch made the thought of its absence into something meaningless.

Before I moved to Chicago for college, Comet Hale-Bopp blazed a thousand times more luminous than Halley's had eleven years earlier, though again I have no memory of seeing its tail, its brightness. I don't remember hearing much about it. My parents never pulled me outside to witness another light sailing through the darkness. The comet's visibility lasted for more than a year and will not return within my lifetime. I suppose by then my parents must have lost all interest in the heavens. That or in the many years since I have simply forgotten them trying to tempt me out again, to stand once more in the weak glow of our kitchen's light as my feet began to fidget.

Of Heaven's Gate, the cult whose mass suicide was widely reported in the wake of Hale-Bopp's appearance, I paid equally little attention. However much the news might have covered thirty-eight people abandoning this world for one they considered a better alternative, I remained oblivious. Even had I known, there was nothing I could have done to stop them from attempting to board a spaceship they believed to have been trailing the comet. Still I like to think that, had I heard what happened, I would have felt sympathetic. Deranged as the cult's leader must have been, I also believe he was sane in knowing he needed healing. His mistake, at least from my perspective, was only in assuming that healing lies beyond this world, this body.

I consider myself fortunate to have learned early on that salvation lies in the opposite direction of the heavens, which are no more capable than our own planet of resisting gravity's depressions. There is no pure life of the spirit as far as I can determine. Lonely are no wiser than happier children. A feeling of isolation does not make you a purer person, only someone who spends too much time examining the husk of things, seeking life amid the lifeless. I once thought I knew how to divorce life from longing, but I was very young then.

Last evening, I met two friends in a hotel lobby where we sipped wine and played board games. I sat to the left of them, both pretty women wearing dresses, when a man with dark hair walked toward me. He seemed both confident and apprehensive, his blue eyes bordering on enormous, his eyelashes long and distracting.

He cleared his throat and asked if I knew how he could get some service, when I told him he had to wait for a waiter to come, to just be patient. He nodded toward the couch opposite and asked if he could take it. I found him attractive, brazen.

I studied him a moment and thought for the first time in ages of the boy I loved when I was seven, a boy whom only a few years later I found conceited, obnoxious. Despite the differences in the ages between the images I held of them both, there was a striking resemblance. When I asked his name after we fell more deeply into conversation, it was the same as the boy I had almost forgotten. The coincidence did not surprise me, however, because of his eyes' burning blueness, because I have now lived long enough to know the same people often come around again, traveling their orbit. When I asked what he was doing here, he said he was meeting a woman he had met online, never yet in person.

Before his date walked in, he showed me photos on his phone of his ceramics. The bulk of his pieces were tea kettles glazed black and cream. It struck me as an unexpected hobby because he looked so muscular, athletic. He leaned in closer and said he lived in a suburb, not the city. Taking a ceramics class was one of few reasons he had, he admitted, for leaving his house on weekday evenings. He had moved here a few months ago from Maryland, hoping for more excitement. He confessed this while knotting his fingers then unlacing them, saying where he lived made sense for his work, though, his company. He asked where I lived, and when I told him, he professed his envy.

At an age when many of my friends are moving to the suburbs for a quieter, more domestic existence, I liked that he laughed when I said a house with children carried the whiff of the end of things. To know your neighbors, to have no way of escaping a life easily predicted, I have long associated with the opposite of living. So many years spent living in a city have all but rid me of my former stoic tendencies, of striving for purity. To know I will never see him again because there are too many lobbies like this, too many other people to whom he bears a vague resemblance, is something I still consider freedom, consider necessary even while married.

When his date walked in, he made space for her on the couch beside him. He hugged her briefly, and they showed each other no more affection, sitting at a strange distance for as long as my friends and I faced them. I thought her blouse unflattering. Pale peach cotton with holes cut through the shoulders, it made her look pregnant. Her voice was pitched at too high a register to last the whole evening without breaking. After she asked him how he knew us and he laughed, admitting he didn't, I turned back to my friends, to our board game.

My friend sitting closest to me finished her wine and whispered that he kept looking our direction. She said he was in love with me, though I am aware she uses that phrase loosely. I know he was merely grateful to find someone to ease his nervousness before meeting another woman. I also left the lobby feeling relieved the dress I was wearing did not suggest I was carrying a baby. I waved goodbye to him with glee at the pain of his existence, his evening. Because of his eyes and their lashes, I felt there was some justice in him living so far from the city, in spending more nights than not wondering if leaving Maryland had been the right decision.

After hugging my friends, I found myself facing a man who lives his life claiming to be a prophet—one of many—haunting the subway. I recognized him from last seeing him when I moved here for college. He did not strike me as having aged as much as might be expected through two decades, perhaps because his hair was gray when I first encountered him, because he has as nearly gray of a complexion. His eyes are still green and ghostly. As with the first time I saw him, he had taken two seats, one for himself and one for his manuscript. Back then, he looked up when I first stepped on the train, when he must have recognized someone in need of saving. I had welcomed his attention then, thinking he saw something others didn't.

I can no longer remember exactly what he told me, but I know he wanted me to buy a copy of the book he'd written. I also know I found him convincing. At the time, I had no money, something I regretted. Still he leaned in close to examine me, to see what we may have had in common. His tongue slid around inside his mouth a bit, and he whispered there was something spiritual about me. He said there was an energy, a willingness to move past all this, as he gestured to the better dressed passengers who were paying very little attention to a man whose clothes smelled of urine and the young woman who needed him. It was only weeks into my first semester, and I already felt a little guilty for not being as pure a person as I had been all my life before this. As bad as the man smelled to me, vacant as his eyes looked as they looked at nothing, part of me also wanted him to save me.

Taking the train home after leaving my friends outside the hotel lobby, he looked up into my face again and recognized me, I felt almost certain. Because the train was crowded, I had no choice except to stand closer to him than I wanted. He looked almost infuriated as he rifled through his wisdom, as he dog-eared pages. His hair was slightly longer, his body thinner than it had been. Though he made no attempt to attract my attention, I also felt he knew I would not listen to him even if he did. He glanced into my face and saw something in me that displeased him. He turned back to those pages promising a life beyond this. He was still enough of a prophet to intuit who would and would not buy and read it.

Late winter, and he was wearing sandals with fraying canvas straps. His feet, his toes were blackened. The rest of his body was covered with thin, easily wrinkled fabric, while he bared his feet to the elements. His pinky toes had no nails left. They were wasting into nothing, as the rest of his feet would continue doing until they vanished. He thought himself capable of transcending all this, and because of his arrogance, I could not bring myself to feel sorry for him. He looked me up and down, maybe remembering how poorly I had been dressed decades earlier, maybe noticing better clothing made little difference.

Another, younger woman asked to sit where his manuscripts rested. To my surprise, he allowed her the privilege. Although she tried looking at her phone, facing away from him, he asked her if she had seen the comet—Lovejoy, he said, the first I had heard of it. I have no idea whether this one will come around again while I'm still living. I doubt, as with all the rest, I will ever see it. He said he asked her because it signaled the world's end, because this was something we should welcome. The woman smiled a little, weakly nodded. He placed his book in her lap, told her this could help carry her to a better life than the one we're living. My stop came. I left the train and walked up the steps to a sky glowing with so many high-rises it never fully darkened.

SPLEEN

CLOUD ELEPHANTS

Earth

There was a strange, sad music to his howling. His voice carried the length of the train when he shouted his sciatica was shooting down his leg. Sciatica, though, was only his way of explaining what Hippocrates diagnosed as black bile pooling in the spleen, what ancient Greeks imagined lay at the root of all melancholy. Even had he explained this, no one would have listened. The four humors are too long lost to science. He smelled too badly.

The train left Manhattan for Queens, and he stuck a finger in his ear. His face became briefly bathed in the erotic as he wriggled his finger more deeply inside his ear's waxen tunnel, as he began living some of his body's private life in public. His finger left its cavern, and his hand reached for his shoulder blade, for a shape grown sharp through hunger yet familiar by palpating.

Sunday afternoon and the train was crowded. Half the passengers were standing. The man's legs started twitching as he begged for a seat. As everyone did their best to ignore him, he stared at my knees, likely noticing both are scar-ridden. Our eyes met, and a part of me felt he needed a stranger not looking away yet also not staring. I felt he needed to be seen with either love or clarity.

He called out to my husband for his seat. My husband sighed then stood and signaled me to stand beside him. I shook my head and stayed seated even as the man sat down, as the woman on my husband's other side left, and her place stayed empty. The man was calm now, however. He kept silent. He rested his elbows against his thighs' slim padding as his spleen began leaching bile blackened by memory. The tattoo of stars encircling his upper arm like a bracelet stopped convulsing in its skin, which was mottled and greasy.

I have seen only one photograph of my maternal grandfather, a photograph that for all I know has long been burned or vanished. Something in this homeless man's features still managed to remind me of him. I know very little concerning him except that he was born into wealth and privilege, except that he last saw my mom on her fourth birthday, not long after my grandmother divorced him. When I was first shown the photograph and realized his features were reflected more softly in my mom's face, she mentioned he'd become a pilot after going to West Point, the military academy. Of their brief marriage, my grandmother said only that he'd spent its bulk flying. Until I saw the man on the train who sat beside me, I had never thought anything more about someone I never had a chance of meeting.

While he was living, not long after his wife became pregnant, he found freedom in the South China Sea as well as other women. Poking the nose of his plane through vast cloud formations while young and handsome, he later died of unknown reasons while my mom was still in college. Wanting to fly again in his next incarnation, riding the subway has now become his only option.

He didn't ask for money. He didn't howl again once his sciatica was soothed by sitting. I watched Manhattan's skyline recede as the subway left the underground's darkness for the sun still blanketing the city. To keep black bile from pooling, to prevent melancholy from overwhelming the system, Hippocrates advised staying in motion. Perhaps without any conscious awareness, this man was obeying ancient wisdom.

He didn't recognize his granddaughter, I was certain. Trying to avoid inhaling the odors that clung to his clothing, I breathed as slowly as I could manage. I breathed from my abdomen then felt myself lighten. I closed my eyes and filled my lungs until they emptied themselves again, until I became briefly conscious of my own skies within, until the crowded subway car felt more spacious. The man stayed still and silent. Sitting beside someone like me, who was slowly becoming more cloud than person, likely appeased the old pilot in him.

When blood is drawn from the body, a dark clot soon settles at the bottom of the vial it is stored in. Some soil looks lodged within the liquid. This is thought to be the basis for the black bile Hippocrates imagined building in the spleen. According to ancient Greek medicine, black bile is blood's densest humor, one of four corresponding to the four elements once considered the basis of all existence. Every human body contains black and yellow bile as well as blood and phlegm. While phlegm contains mostly water and fire lends yellow bile its coloring, black bile is weighted with the earth's darkness. Health depends on keeping these four humors in balance.

Some melancholy—some black bile to keep the yellow's heat from turning the skin jaundiced—in other words is needed. Without some earth in our systems, we would all become pilots. The planet would be left unattended. We would live out our lives among clouds grown large as elephants, floating among the largest of animal species, only to change into another animal far too quickly. We would too soon inhabit a heaven, ascending to a cloud realm that I am far from certain is really heaven.

After my husband and I stepped off the train, I picked a white tulip at the airport's entrance. I pulled the flower out with its roots still connected to its stem. My husband shot me a look, asking why I did this. I said I had no reason, acknowledging I simply had an impulse and followed it. I had nowhere to put this flower, whose roots and dirt attached seemed excessive. Before we walked inside, I dropped the tulip onto another flower bed. I dropped it, and the blossom flattened against soil in which several others were planted. Its roots wriggled toward the sky. They were straggling toward clouds, indifferent to everything taking place below them. Brown roots pulled from the ground too are homeless. Seeing the clouds in motion likely does nothing for them.

Water

WHEN TWO people stand or sit beside each other without speaking, sometimes too much happens for either one to want to know each other more closely. Inhabiting their separate skins, parts of them go swimming. The water inside them begins to ripple before leaping over stones it also smoothens. Strangers as much to each other as everyone else standing dry around them, they alone share the sense that they are reaching their arms forward into air, wafting in waves being pulled toward no ocean.

However long it had been since the homeless man had performed any ablutions, he may still have been born in water for all I knew to the contrary. His mother may still have birthed him in a pool in which he paddled with fingers too small to yet grasp anything solid. Outside the pool, life ever afterward to him may have seemed less fluid. Deep within his spleen, he may have felt something had gone wrong with him.

From LaGuardia, we were returning to Chicago after a long weekend. My husband pointed to my skirt, which was whitened now in blotches. He shook his head at stains resembling toothpaste patches. He said the man's pants were coated with bird shit and I had sat too close to him. I didn't have to be clean to fly so long as I had my ticket, I riposted. I could sit throughout the flight as if I were as rooted in the earth as a young tulip.

Of all the body's organs, the spleen is the only one commonly compared to a paperback in size and weight. I read this once in a book bound in hardcover and found the description consoling, the fact I might hold it in my hand and read it while flying over the ocean. Only what the paperback might say as to suffering's origin—why some earth in the blood weights us with unhappiness—these books keep silent.

Less than a year after my mom was buried not far from the small Indiana town she was born in, my husband and I flew to the French Riviera, where I sunbathed topless and no one noticed because every other woman enjoyed the same freedom. Each day in the bathroom of the room we rented, I found ants plundering the bristles of my toothbrush. I rinsed it in hot water that still left in some black limbs. I went swimming in the cool Mediterranean.

A man we met bicycling suggested we visit a village known for being the origin of the Sorgue, the most sparkling river in the region. Although the river seems to spring from beneath a cliff, its true origin remains mysterious. Hundreds of explorers spanning centuries have created conduits to find its genesis. Hundreds of divers have swum deep down below the earth's surface, yet none has found it.

Still it is a river flowing like all others into an ocean. Its wellspring may be buried beyond finding, but it still produces water so clear it seemed to me to be a living presence. This is what comes of water emerging from such pure darkness. Water this shining, water resembling joy made fluid, is what comes of contact with melancholy so concentrated it has gone into hiding.

Late afternoon, and my husband and I ordered fish from a café overlooking the river. I bit into the fish, forgetting that restaurants in Europe do not debone them and swallowed a few bones in the process. I swallowed them and almost stopped breathing for a moment. I gasped for air and suddenly understood that my mom had been born again as water this shimmering. She had decayed into the earth, then swum from out the soil with the same speed as a train leaving its underground labyrinth.

I spat out a few bones into my napkin. With my fork, I peeled back the flesh of the fish more carefully from its skeleton and realized she had become the one element she was often missing, more than likely to rectify the imbalance. I thought of her taking baths on only a weekly basis, of her going to work unwashed nearly every morning. She also drank very little water, surviving largely on diet cola and coffee. After her divorce, my grandmother had become an alcoholic, and much of my mom's hygiene had gone unattended as a consequence. She once confessed she often went to school wearing unlaundered clothing. Had she been with me in New York City, she may have minded the odor of the man on the train less than the average person. She may have minded sitting beside him even less than I did.

Her body's cleanliness was always less important to her than keeping clean within, than holding no resentment. Even as a child, she told me she was always conscious of the need to forgive both her parents, to keep an inner space empty, her inner skies from clouding. I believe this is what allowed her to love my sister and me freely, to give us nightly baths and regularly wash our clothing. When I attempt to describe her goodness, I am aware people rarely believe me, thinking I've exaggerated. I have largely abandoned attempting to describe her for this reason.

She laughed extremely easily. She was very pretty without trying to be. In this and other ways, I hardly resemble her. I struggle instead to sit quietly while my spleen leaches black fluid into my stomach and intestines. I often feel I am burning rather than flowing like pellucid water through a bucolic French village. In addition to having eyes not brown but green, her build was also slighter. Her face had a far more delicate bone structure. She herself was not a farmer's but a pilot's daughter.

Air

CLOUD ELEPHANTS bewitched those living in the Himalayas in long-gone centuries. These vaporous beings seemed to float above ground made cooler by their passing. Yet only those who take the time to notice the sky can ever witness them. See something moving as slowly as breath exhaled from the abdomen and melancholy lessens. The earth surrenders some of its reality to the heavens.

One of the friends I visited in New York City had recently moved to a new apartment, one where her young son's bedroom leads out onto a terrace. One of his walls is made of glass, which slides back to reveal a wooden floor covered by a Turkish carpet and with only sky for ceiling. Late into the evening, my friend and I sat across from her flower boxes, drinking wine and reminiscing about when we were much younger women. She asked me whether I remembered when we used to ride in the bed of my dad's pickup to the lake where my parents liked to waterski. I smiled and nodded.

The first time I invited her to this lake in the middle of Midwestern corn country, I told her we would ride on lawn chairs in the pickup's bed during the hour's drive there. I had said it to her as if this made us women of leisure, as if we were leaving for a holiday on the Mediterranean. My enthusiasm for this ease of living, she said, had touched her.

When we were done waterskiing and swimming, we rode home in the truck's bed again. On the way back, we folded the lawn chairs down. We lay on beach towels against the truck's steel rivets, which were hard and uncomfortable, she remembered. This way, however, we could see the clouds changing. We could see their white tails lengthen then blossom.

As my friend recounted this, she looked up toward a skyline littered with too many lights from too many apartments for there to be any stars left. Though there was no wind on her terrace, her face looked windswept. I kept silent but remembered how I had enjoyed this part of the trip less than she did. I had liked sitting in lawn chairs rather than lying on towels and shivering, looking up at clouds continually shape shifting so that I could never know whether any animals actually inhabited them.

I finished my wine and told her I was growing chilly on the terrace. We went inside and watched aerial shots of American landscapes set to classical music. We watched the channel to which the TV was already set without changing it. We watched Yellowstone's geysers then more of Montana's big sky country, a place neither she nor I have ever been, and a place she acknowledged she has no desire to visit. This did not surprise me given that she herself is airy, and all things must be kept in balance. Only I said I might someday want to see a place so expansive. I said this without being sure if I meant it. Whenever I fly places, I rarely turn my head from my paperback before a plane has landed.

Doctors have considered the spleen a vestigial organ for centuries, simply because we can live without it. They have seen little use for melancholy, having long dismissed Hippocrates's wisdom. The list of organs we are thought to have evolved beyond as a species while retaining them was once much longer than at present. We have slowly worked our way through the list, discovering that we need a good number of them. The myth has persisted only because we demanded far less of our bodies until we began living to older ages.

It was not until 2007 that scientists confirmed the spleen can help heal a heart that's nearly broken. The spleen's white blood cells alone, they discovered through several studies, can devour dying heart tissue, can keep this tissue from contaminating what remains healthy. The white lurking inside the bile's blackness assists the heart in recovering from disease that otherwise could kill the whole organism. Only the healing that comes of melancholy allows this. The heart can love again only through some infiltration of sadness.

Live only to your forties, however, and heart disease is usually not a problem. No one living at the time of Hippocrates survived long enough to discover the healing properties of a melancholy organ. No one then read books made from paper, only vellum. No one in ancient times had the luxury of forgetting life's impermanence. I have rarely seen animals in clouds for this reason, because one species morphs into another too quickly. A cloud loses a tail one moment, and the next the curl of an eyelash becomes a larger appendage.

Yet elephants are clouds, and clouds are elephants in essence. Inside a Chelsea museum dedicated to the art of the Himalayas, a piece of metalwork from Nepal depicts an elephant whose tail widens into a flower of its same silver coloring. The plaque beside it claims this rain blossom was once part of a Sanskrit text in which a king and his subjects debated whether elephants were still elephants once their bodies filled with air and floated. Were elephants still animals once they became clouds? The kingdom considered this. On the plaque, no answer to the question was provided.

Only once the monsoon comes to Nepal, elephants begin dancing. This is fact, not legend. Relief washes over them as the heat comes to an end. They lift their heavy legs and flap their ears while blowing water out their trunks. At each change of season, this happens regardless of what occupies their counterparts in the heavens. The rains are something earthly elephants have ample reason to celebrate, as they are unable to sweat through their leathery skins, as splashing themselves with mud remains their only means of self-cooling. Elephants know as well as anyone there can be too much heat, too much of any one element.

And as the rains come and elephants bathe again, they appear whiter than they had been. Shorn of mud baked into their pores over too many hot months on end, they briefly look as incandescent as any cloud with the sun flashing behind it. Walking through jungle and forest, they seem to shimmer for a moment. Flattening the grass beneath their feet, they seem to flow as gently as a river, filling their lungs with air too thin to remain long inside them.

Elephants too tend to move slowly. Cloud elephants seem to do the same until you study them. Only then do you see they don't live long enough for us to recognize them as a species. They reveal no internal organs once you slice them open. They never sicken with disease when one of the body's four humors is lacking or excessive, throwing the entire system off balance. When their sciatica flairs with pain, they have no need for sitting. Instead, they thin then vanish.

Fire

BECAUSE WE lived as far from town as we did, more than ten miles from the nearest post office or grocery, my mom burned our garbage most evenings after we'd eaten. She walked softly past my bedroom, barefoot throughout summer, spring, and early autumn. She padded past where my bed lay level with the windowsill, where I often read while looking out onto our orchard and garden. At the orchard's end was a cylinder of fence, inside which we tossed anything we no longer needed. My mom ritually lit a small fire there as the sun was setting.

My parents never lit any logs inside our fireplace, however. Doing so, they always claimed, made the electric heat escape out the flue of the chimney. They said the heat from a fire was inefficient when I voiced my desire to see flames rising toward the heavens. I therefore equated fire less with heat than as a way of ridding ourselves of what we were done with, of keeping our house and yard from smelling. And fire may still rid the earth of garbage, but neither this nor any other element can bring back something that has vanished. Not a single one of them can make a river turn back into a woman.

Our last afternoon in New York City, before I met my grandfather's reincarnation on the subway, I saw a man melting. A man wearing only white underwear and pinching his belly stood on the High Line and reached his arms out in what appeared both pain and longing. Walking beside my husband, I laughed and pointed. He stood so still and yet looked impassioned, desperate for either love or clarity. I could not keep from laughing because he was revealing so much of his body.

The man was made of wax, however, something I saw only once I came closer. Seeing I had mistaken him for a human, my husband laughed yet more loudly, because this is a pattern with me. Because I want everything to be living. Because instead of death's resolution, I believe in the four elements recombining themselves into another river or person.

If the man standing there nearly naked only had a wick on the crown of his head, I could have lit him. Yet the sun was doing some of the work for me, diminishing both his stature and his longing. Still with a lighter and a wick I could have shortened his lifespan. I could have watched fire burn from his head, which looked too cleanly shaven for hair to have ever grown there to begin with.

Each time my mom burned our garbage, I realize now she must have burned some of herself along with it. She must have burned the farthest stretch of her fingertips. She must have burned some of the cilia lining her nostrils, then her elbows until they became rounded. She burned little by little of herself, small parts of her neck and her kidneys and her wrists. Her navel and her pubis and finally her spleen were incinerated. Her heart dried to ashes. Because my resemblance to her is so slight, because she was so slim and pretty, I will likely live longer than necessary while she did the opposite.

Hippocrates's theory of the four humors has no basis in modern science. Only if melancholy does not reside within the body, does not inhabit a particular organ, it must still live somewhere. No one disputes its existence. Regardless of its origin, it still affects us, some more than others. If it does not arise from one of the four humors, it still falls on some of us as heavily as the monsoon that sets the elephants dancing.

Inside LaGuardia, after my husband and I passed through security, a man brushed past me. Young and handsome, he was nearly running as he went our opposite direction. He carried a bouquet of red roses. Though symbolic of love burning inside him, in truth they were dying since the moment someone plucked them. My husband saw me watching him and sniffed, asking me if roses were something I wanted. We were traveling, I responded. Even if he bought me any, I had no vase to put them in. I reminded him I had already killed a tulip.

Closer to our gate, another man stood behind a table asking everyone who passed him to buy vitamins. Each bottle had a picture of a celebrity, a woman who looked ageless. I do not want to be this woman. I do not even want my blood and phlegm and yellow bile to put the black bile in balance. All I want is to continue burning until I am finished. Still looking toward the vitamins, I also realized I was carrying some of the stench of the man who had sat beside me on the subway. I became conscious of the need to burn the garbage, something likely not allowed in New York City.

Although I looked away from the man selling the vitamins, he still shouted to me to try them. He said they acted as a life extension while the man carrying the roses rushed past me, brushing my side again, this time approaching from behind, only more quickly. There was something he had either left or forgotten. Or perhaps he only wanted to fly to another city and visit another woman. His roses were already wilting, something I could see from their edges, while the vitamin salesman kept trying to attract my attention. Try again, I turned and told him, knowing he had no way of knowing what I meant. Try and breathe and open the skies within. Watch the elephants' tails blossom.

SINUSES

SKULL CATHEDRAL

A few months before my sister became pregnant, our dad walked up wooden stairs we never varnished. Years ago, he had overlaid them with rubber carpet instead. In this way and without intending it, he softened his own footsteps as he left our basement, as he approached an anteroom that led inside our kitchen. While we sat warmed by the nearness of the oven, he opened the door and stood beside the sink, his day of farming finished. He washed his hands and cast a tall shadow across the floor as wild cats crept among those ferns lining our house's foundation, as the sun sank behind our rhubarb patches. Although this was likely never his objective, the stairs' rubber skin made his presence less expected than it should have been. It made a house whose quiet was always a holiness yet more sacred.

He had been dead a couple of years, buried level with and several miles from our basement, when he started walking up these stairs again. He was heard, I was told, in the evenings most often.

He was heard leaving a place of circuit breakers and cobwebs for a kitchen smelling of soap and butter and bread. For months, he shook the house with his movements. He made some small thunder in the basement with the heft that clung to him even in death, yet he never came back inside the kitchen. He never saw any more green tomatoes ripening on the window ledge, never noticed how we moved the refrigerator closer to the pie cabinet. I suppose he tried to twist the doorknob open. Without a hand, though, he could never manage.

At the time, my sister and I were leasing our farmhouse to Mia, one of my sister's closest childhood friends. Only a few years before this, the house's collapsing white trellises were weighted with still whiter clematis. Not long after Mia moved in, the porch's foundation began to split. Forks of black lightning sprouted with weeds, though I doubt she ever noticed. Weekdays, she taught art to young children while in the evenings, sitting cross-legged on her bed or our living room carpet, she felt pockets of energy around her shift and knew them to be human. A vegan who braided her own hemp bracelets, she looked unnaturally thin among southern Indiana's carnivorous and corn-fed. She had moved back to the Midwest from Arizona, where she went to college, a couple years after graduation.

From spending the night at our house for so many years on end, Mia remembered several of my dad's habits. She knew how in the early evenings he opened the wooden latch to a door opposite a pole attached to clotheslines strung across an herb garden. She knew from there he descended to the basement. Encased within its darkness, he walked past a wardrobe inherited from his parents and undid his boot-laces. He scraped dirt from his soles with a pocketknife as he sat on the stairs beside the furnace. From a floor above him, we often heard a soft scratching sounding like a bat wanting in—the susurrus of his broom against cement.

When Mia signed her lease, I was working for a magazine in Chicago, five hours north of where my dad was growing restive in the basement. The magazine advocated for the rescue of shelter pets and was under constant threat of going out of business. Our small staff was frequently issued late paychecks. When someone was fired or quit, no one replaced them. Most days, I wrote about puppy mills and campaigns to neuter feral kittens. I worked from a desk so near Chicago's L tracks that passing trains shook our office. When Mia told us that my dad was stirring, trying to reach the kitchen, this changed nothing for me. She offered me no solace, as she likely intended. Writing in the voice of animals in need of adoption, doubting Mia's contact with another dimension, I found myself wondering instead if our kitchen wallpaper had begun to peel yet, if the faded cornucopia baskets spilling their apples at last had fallen.

It was early spring when Mia moved in. Once the Indiana summer came around again, she went without air conditioning. She more than likely could not afford it, but she also kept most of the windows closed in the heat, my sister reported from her many visits. It was as if she were trying to recreate the Arizona climate in a place where the heat was never arid. In her thinness, surviving on little more than those few plants she grew in our garden, Mia didn't seem to feel the same discomfort others would have while sweating beneath the shade of my mom's curtains. My sister said the house had begun to smell by early August. She suspected mold, asked me if I thought this could be it. I stayed silent, leaving her to answer her own question as I imagined the humidity ungluing the apples on the wallpaper further from their horn-shaped baskets.

At work, I left the fates of dogs and cats no one wanted unstated. After listing their ages and sexes, I said nothing as to their coming deaths should no one adopt them in order to make the ads more persuasive. Seeing little reason for delaying their next incarnation, seeing less for spending much time with friends outside the office, in our apartment I read lengthy passages of *The Tibetan Book of the Dead* aloud to my husband. I read that dreams of having your head wrapped in a red silk turban, of eating feces, of wearing clothes sewn from the hides of yaks, all prognosticated an imminent death, among other omens. Yet the bardo remained its focus. The liminal dimension hovering between lifetimes, between embodiments.

After the body lies still and lifeless, after the heart has beat its last, the luminous splendor of the colorless light of emptiness reveals itself only briefly to the emerging consciousness. Within the first few moments of death, every one of us encounters its salvation. The light's concentration causes most to turn away and face the relief of the darkness instead, to miss transcendence. We then find ourselves forced into another round of birth and death, another incarnation. Only before this happens, our consciousness alone begins to wander a world catering only to the senses in what are said to be the bardo's final stages. Considerable pain ensues in this.

The Tibetan Book of the Dead likens our last moments in this dimension to walking the desert with a terrible thirst and no water to slake it. All the flesh's pleasures become manifest, though consciousness alone cannot enjoy them. Baskets overspill with apples, yet you have no tongue to taste, no stomach to digest them. Both animals and humans begin to fill the space where the colorless light of emptiness has now vanished. They appear from every vantage, and all are having sex. All are reaching orgasm. They thicken the air with desire you begin to throb with even while bodiless. Walking too near them—trying to insert yourself between two locked in coitus—only makes you become one of their children.

Even here, though, there are options. The longer you resist the urge to slip between a pair of hips, the more control you exercise over your next incarnation. The more suffering you sustain between lifetimes, watching sex without having it, the less suffering you are likely to face when reborn in another body, at least according to Tibetan Buddhists. Making peace with emptiness while still living prepares you for this challenge. Hours spent sitting cross-legged on the floor, doing nothing, help you to withstand the coming agony, to choose better parents even if you do turn away from the light again. The bardo, however, comes to some of us early. Those whose lives are flush with sweetness, whose evenings teem with fruit filling cornucopia baskets, know of emptiness only in theory.

When I visited Mia with my sister around Christmas, she made us green tea sweetened with honey. I noticed she had overhung the living room chandelier with pine branches whose needles were falling in sparse, brown rain that pricked the carpet. Tungsten inside bulbs shaped into tulips had long frayed into nothing, and Mia lit the room with beeswax candles instead. Autumn leaves still blanketed our yard's expanses. They had compacted into mulch where my sister and I once played badminton. They swelled into cysts beneath the magnolia tree that once held the Easter Bunny's purple eggs my mom had hidden. The grass wouldn't grow until next spring, though, even if we raked them.

We finished the pot of tea and switched to a bottle of Tuscan red. After a few glasses, sitting on the floor in the lotus position, Mia said she considered my dad a companion, here in a house more than ten miles from the nearest grocery or post office. He was stirring more now, though, than he had been. He still thought he had a body, she added. He was acting on its memories, though even these seemed to sense his work day had ended. He was ready to walk back inside the kitchen, to rest from his exertions. This was not, she said, a stage that lasted.

After Christmas and as winter deepened, the footsteps dissolved into silence. They never started again. My dad stopped trying to walk back inside our kitchen. Spring came earlier than expected, and torrents flooded our driveway, keeping Mia stranded. Newborn lakes and rivers overspreading our pastures' grasses forced her to call off work for three days while eating more of next to nothing than she normally did. The waters rose as well inside my sister's basement. She walked down her stairs carrying a mop and vomited. Her husband began noticing her labored movements.

For a time, before the flooding, the mold receded. It was absorbed by ice that clung onto drainpipes and window frames that were rarely opened during summer. For a few months, the mold seemed to vanish only to resurge once Mia moved back to Arizona. She said she missed the red rock formations, the climate, her old boyfriend, with whom she was going to try to make things work again.

The mold's metastasis forced us to take up the carpet before we could rent the house to another tenant. My dad had lived here all his life except for four years in college—his parents had given him the house upon his marriage—and the mold's sudden spread must have bothered him. It must have been as much a catalyst in his surrender to a pair of thrusting hips as the agony of watching bodies climax in the basement, where the bardo had temporarily been. He would have wanted us to take better care of the home he had left as our inheritance, the home where neither my sister nor I could stand to live because our memories clung as tightly to its walls as cornucopia baskets with only paper fruit inside them.

My sister began sewing soft, woolen blankets. She painted her nursery green for either sex of baby as my husband and I packed all our possessions into boxes. Our lease was ending, and we were moving to a smaller, less expensive apartment. My husband had taken a job that earned less money, and my boss still made late payments. As Mia left the mold to wreak its damage, as my sister negotiated with contractors about its removal with her swelling belly, my husband and I vacated a high-rise for a garden unit without a garden. The windows of our new living room were half filled with dirt in which no trees or flowers were rooted. Before the movers came to our old unit, I gave away several small tables and lamps, bags of clothing. I kept only a few shoeboxes of keepsakes from my parents—an old watch, birthday cards, and hospital bracelets—so our space would seem less crowded. Our new lives would be lived half within a basement.

From inside our new living room, we looked out onto a street flush with legs and feet. There were far too many for me not to want to see their faces, not to want to take long and longer walks without my husband to see whether our eyes would meet. Our building was wedged between a dry cleaner and a shoe repair shop with an awning I suspected of molding. We faced a palm reader across the street. I often tried looking away from the neon sign with an eye at hand's center but found I couldn't because it was always watching. All three places of business were also housed within garden units. The earth had claimed us all too early. It made us walk the bardo while we were still living. Perhaps the dry cleaner, shoe repairman, and palm reader didn't share this realization. At the time, however, I needed the illusion of sympathy, someone else who understood what it was to practice dying.

Both the shoe repairman and dry cleaner were men who looked in their later forties, both with hair graying on the sides in patches. Early evenings, I smiled and waved near their entryways as my shadow lengthened, as they sat behind their counters for a few more hours while I read or watched TV. Both filled their window-sills with small cacti and succulents. In milder weather, they kept their doors open, and I heard classical music streaming from their storefronts. In the mornings once I left our kitchen and walked up a few steps to stand level with the street, I could see their radios sitting sentient, their hands working nimbly with thread. From inside our apartment, my husband could see only the lower half of my body. I always left for work earlier than he did.

I never walked inside either place of business, never gave either man any of my money. I cleaned all my clothes in a washing machine and wore only shoes not worth repairing. Still, both struck me as quiet, almost sacred places. Had I only a sweater with a stain on its sleeve and enough extra money to pay for dry cleaning—had I a shoe with a heel broken—they could have done something. As it was, they seemed holier to me for repairing nothing real, only shoes and clothing.

Sometimes I imagined them stroking my hair in rhythm with their classical music when I was trying to fall asleep. They would braid it then serve me the tea I often saw them sipping. I also knew we would all be flooded if a large enough storm came. We would be the first to be washed away into the ocean. The eye at hand's center outside the palm reader would loom over us all as we started drowning, as we were buried by water and met the colorless light of emptiness together, as we felt ourselves healed by its terrible splendor. We lay closer to the truth of things than all those swinging their arms and legs above us. This was our advantage. We were half dead, half buried, already. Their glowing, expressionless faces behind their glass doors were necessary for me. Only now do I see this. Their softly parted lips, their succulents kept in clear, round vases. Though I thought myself at peace with my own emptiness, I also wanted someone to see me waving.

My sister's water broke, and my nephew came into the world a couple pounds smaller than expected. In utero, the umbilical cord had wrapped itself around his neck, something that would have presented more problems had he been born only a few days later, my sister told me. What had fed him for nine months also slowly strangled him without even the doctor knowing. Because I had made no attempt to be present at the birth, my sister told me this over the phone rather than in person. Standing there alone beside the hospital bed, I imagined I could do nothing for either one of them, for mother or infant. From Arizona, Mia texted her congratulations.

I came home one evening and noticed time had reversed itself to the 1930s. A movie was being filmed near our apartment. Beneath the floodlights, with its owner paid to leave his building, the shoe repair shop looked older than I had ever seen it as women slender as Mia wearing waistless dresses walked past, smiling and indifferent to those inhabiting another century. With their heels sounding like nails being pounded into pavement, they spoke to each other more naturally for speaking from a script. The nearby movie theater and pharmacy were given wider windows and curtains. A trolley stood in the center of the street, which was closed for days to traffic. Leaving for work one morning, I caught my best glimpse of the starring actor and actress, both with smooth skin and eyes wide as fish, both looking much smaller than they do on screen.

My husband and I ate dinner in a nearby tavern where a bluegrass band was playing the night filming finished. The world surrounding our apartment returned to the present, and three men wearing leather vests strummed guitars on a stage with crepe paper overhanging its edges. At first, I paid little attention. I was tired from the work week, from saving too many animals from deaths that would only come again after they were adopted. I didn't know until a song called "After Midnight" started how much I had needed for these three men to sing in unison about a married woman sleeping in another man's bed, how much I had needed to drink a glass of wine while sitting across from my husband, for us to dance a while with our arms wrapped around each other's necks and shoulders. When the woman in the song left, she created a cavern in the mattress. She left one place empty so someone else could fill it. The song made something sweet out of emptiness.

The lead singer's hair was silver and wavy. From a short distance, it became a bed of soap bubbles filling a bath I wanted to be taking. He looked to be fifteen or more years older than me, and from the stage he asked me to take the tip jar around the tables after the second set was finished. He complimented my dress when I handed the jar back to him. He dedicated the last song to the woman who had helped fill his pockets, saying with everyone else in the tavern hearing that this was the beginning of a love affair for him. Only since the affair had started in public, it couldn't be a secret, he whispered into the microphone yet more loudly. Playing some chords before another song started, he offered his apologies to my husband.

A few weekends later, we saw the same band again. My husband would have rather stayed in, he mentioned before we left, would have rather read or watched a movie. The lead singer's weathered beauty, the attention he paid me, telling me I looked lovely when I walked in behind my husband, was all an accident, I realized even then. Still I felt myself changed by it. I felt myself ripen like a green tomato set in the sun on a window ledge. I worked too many hours at the pet magazine in silence without caring whether the animals were adopted not to come alive with the attention. A subtle and quiet reincarnation.

My senses too were hungry. Until I turned my head toward the darkness, until I swayed to sad and tinny music in the shadows of the tavern, I hadn't known this, however. I had looked too long at light that was both empty and colorless. For the first time in several years on end, I became aware of my body. The gaze of an older man who could be considered handsome fell warm on my shoulders, softening them as well as all the muscles connecting to my coccyx, making my spine into a languid river. Since the death of my dad and my mom not long before him, my husband had seen me as too wounded for much sexual aggression. I read aloud too many lengthy passages from *The Tibetan Book of the Dead* for him to forget my preoccupation with another dimension. Like the time before this, the lead singer asked me to pass the tip jar after the second set was finished. When I handed it full of bills to him, he said now he could eat again. Without me, he would starve, be famished.

There is a carnality, I realized then, that lies buried deep within the sacred. There is lust that thickens the air filling even holy places. Every cathedral has benches from which to gaze on beautiful men and women. The hollows inside my head, which the lead singer now haunted, were no different. I became aware of him roaming my skull's open spaces, my eardrums, my sinuses, those cavities forming the shape of a butterfly for no known reason. Yet once the heart stops beating, consciousness needs a means of escaping to another realm, a liminal one of pure spirit. The butterfly of my sinuses may be as good a place as any. The skull's cathedral may be a sacred place to pray for transcendence. It is also a place to leave when you are ready.

At the end of each weekday, after walking a few steps down to my kitchen, I made dinner knowing I was living in the bardo's final stages. I paid the dry cleaner and shoe repairman less attention, stopped smiling and waving as often. In the full light of day, I saw every attractive man more clearly for the one I'd seen only in darkness, because it was always after midnight when the bluegrass band finished playing. I bought myself new clothes, waiting to walk back inside the tavern wearing pants, dresses, and blouses that better fit me. Meanwhile the eye at hand's center across the street never blinked, kept watching.

My sister called and told me Mia had broken up with her boyfriend. This time, she wasn't leaving Arizona again. She had found Indiana too flat, too humid. My sister never told her the mold was a problem. My nephew's crawling now seemed more important. In his new incarnation, my dad's brown eyes had lightened to blue. When he slept, his bottom lip slipped sideways. He had begun gurgling, trying to make conversation, trying to tell me how he had wrestled with the bardo's eroticism for far longer than average. I spent hours on my sister's couch with him, trying to listen, trying to hear him explain through his mewling how he had stayed there long enough to return the only way possible to his family. He had to wait for my sister to have surgery removing polyps from her uterus. Never having wanted children, I provided him no opening. I have been on birth control now for decades.

My husband grew tired of going to the same tavern each weekend. He knew the reason we went so often, complained about hearing the same songs sung again, the tip jar routine the lead singer perfected. He told me to stop buying new clothing. We didn't have room in our closet unless we moved to another apartment. I did as he wanted but started working from home on a freelance basis. Having grown tired of pretending I wanted to save things that were clearly dying, I quit the pet magazine.

For certain ceremonies, Tibetan Buddhists drink from a human skull known as a kapala. They pay homage to deities whom they hope will help them withstand the bardo's agony, to make wiser choices regarding their next incarnation if not surrender to the colorless light of emptiness entirely. The skull is intricately carved and overlaid with jewelry. In many ancient paintings, beloved deities hold a kapala flush with lapidary beauty. They quaff human blood, according to tradition. Monks, however, often fill their kapalas with cakes instead. They bake them to resemble human eyes, ears, and tongues—all the skull has dispensed with in death, those fragile portals of the senses—then place them at skull's bottom. They fall asleep waiting for deities to devour these symbols of impermanence so their bodies' desires cannot in turn devour them.

I have never seen a kapala in person, have never seen a human skull outside a natural history museum. But I can easily imagine my own head filled with eyes and ears and tongues, those cut from and belonging to another body, instead of the thoughts that tend to fill it. Normally the eyes, ears, and tongues taste of dough sweetened with honey, of dough growing harder the longer it lies uneaten. A man I found myself briefly almost loving seemed to make the promise of more sweetness in this life an option. It was only the promise, though, I needed.

By the time we moved apartments again, the band no longer performed at the same tavern. The band no longer existed once we moved to a third-story unit where we sat level with the city's forest canopy. I received the news from an e-newsletter the lead singer sent to hundreds. There had never been any real temptation for me to resist in the bardo when I was living half within a basement. There had been only suggestions in the song lyrics. Still, I stopped reading *The Tibetan Book of the Dead* aloud to my husband. I derived too much pleasure now from the senses, had bought too much new clothing. In my new neighborhood, where we have remained now for years on end, there are dry cleaners and shoe repair shops, all only a couple stories below me. They sit level with the street. Those men who work their lives away inside them do not seem friendly.

There is more light, as well as noise, in this building. The windows stretch nearly to the ceiling, and the walls are thin. My husband and I often hear our neighbors having sex, rarely with the same people, as I imagine. We are likely the only people here who are married, whose sex is mostly quiet. I still work from home, still on a freelance basis. Many of those living in the units around me are also home on weekdays for unknown reasons. They shake the walls with their lovemaking and their music, which goes quiet only in the evening.

A couple months ago, I went alone to a movie. Walking inside the theater near sunset, I confronted a familiar silhouette. It was the bluegrass band's bassist. He noticed me studying his profile, which always struck me as handsome. He hugged and introduced me to his girlfriend, confessing he hadn't played music in ages. They were leaving the same movie I was seeing, and he told me it was sadder than all the previews led him to believe. His girlfriend noticed the dress I was wearing, one I had bought for the lead singer to notice but he had never seen. She told me it was pretty. I had not bought it for other women, had bought it for nothing.

The lead singer had gotten tired of all the late evenings, the bassist said when I asked him why things ended. His hair's soap bubbles were bursting. He had wanted more time to spend with his wife on weekends. They wanted to do more traveling, had recently left for a month to see the northern lights from the top of Norway, the bassist added, laughing. I realized then he must have never really needed the tips I gave him, must have always had plenty of money. He must have only pretended to be hungry.

THIRD
EYELID

RUNNING THROUGH WATER

She was only my invention from the beginning. For years, I held out hope of becoming this other woman, this goddess I have long felt stirring inside me. Eventually, I accepted this would never happen. She was nothing more than my personal religion, which I have known better than to believe in now for decades but continue paying homage. I still sense her swimming through my gallbladder, my kidneys when the world becomes liquid, when I spend the evening sitting in the tub until my fingertips resemble pale raisins. Below any body of water's surface, she again breathes through my lungs, dissolves like an aspirin through my bloodstream. I step out of the bath, taste salt on my lips. I dry myself with a towel, knowing she has vanished.

Not long after I joined the swim team, I stood before my parents' bedroom mirror, extending tall from their dresser. I slipped out of my cotton dress and into my mom's bikini, which was the color of an olive. Outside in our garden, my parents were harvesting green beans and cabbage, both too busy to wonder what I was doing. Lengthening my neck toward the ceiling, I held my breath, stretched my arms out and pretended I was sculling through air thickening into fluid. I practiced being the goddess.

Exhaling, I tied the bikini top's straps more tightly around my back. Leaning across the dresser and fogging the mirror with my breath, I folded my stomach over the drawer where my dad kept handkerchiefs. I searched my pupils for the small stars whose light implied vast distance and told me of the goddess's presence. I looked inside my own body's darkness with the appetite of a beggar needing money, waiting for the light to reach me. I fell deeply in love with my own becoming.

Within a few more years, I became such a disappointment in comparison to what I had imagined, a woman whose beauty could attract love without limits. My only consolation was pretending the goddess came to life once I started swimming from one side of the pool and back again, which was as good a reason as any to stay on the team while winning no races, while only half hiding beneath the water's blanket. Only most of my life was lived outside the water. Most of my life, I had more trouble imagining I was someone different than I seemed. In my drier moments, I believed the goddess had abandoned me for the Sea Gypsies, those who make a home of the ocean, who daily search the water's bottom for sea slugs, for mollusks. Even now, I can hardly blame them for stealing her away from me without knowing.

Those few Sea Gypsies still in existence inhabit the Andaman Sea's coastal islands. Known as Moken, they can hold their breath for up to five minutes before breaching the waves without gasping. They catch fish with their hands and kick through the blueness to a beach where a fire illumines a shipwreck's flotsam. They fall asleep among nests of seaweed as the goddess blows cool air onto their faces before they waken with sea-bloated bellies. Unlike myself, they have tried to keep swimming.

For thousands of years, they have lived as nomads among beaches now metastasizing with high-rises, with bleak and silver gas stations. The governments of Malaysia, Myanmar, and Thailand have coaxed the Moken into their homes, shops, and prisons. They have restricted their hunting grounds to waters surrounding smaller islands. Thousands have been forced onto national parklands, where they are made to serve as tourist attractions. Yet however far they are kept from the ocean, some part of me wants to believe not everything can be taken away. Even when they can no longer swim to catch the fish that once sustained them, I want to believe they can also sense a goddess flowing through their bloodstream.

All life evolves from the sea into dryness. Life is nothing if not a progressive loss of moisture from hair, from skin, from the mucus lining our orifices even as the earth's water level rises. The years pass. Spines bend, muscles weaken. The oils smoothing your skin congeal into something nearly solid as you come closer to forgetting how near you once were to becoming a goddess. No one may have glimpsed her beauty, yourself included. Still she swims through your veins, your arteries once you go swimming.

Kicking their legs through turquoise inlets, those few tribes of Moken who remain say nothing of their way of life's end. They hold their breath instead, keep silent. They slow their already languid movements while seeing underwater as well as dolphins. They constrict their pupils and flex their eyes' lenses, an ability scientists have demonstrated belongs to all children. It is only the need that is missing. Most children do not need to hunt below the sea as a matter of survival. All we see clearly, scientists have determined, is that which keeps us from starving. The goddess for me has then gone largely missing because I have lost a certain amount of moisture in my hair and skin. I have adapted to a life with less beauty than I once imagined. The goddess herself may now be dry, shriveled and wizened, but finding her still feels important.

In Chicago, I walk most evenings along Lake Michigan. The world is darkness once I reach my apartment after my workday is finished. Even before daylight fades into nothing, there are too many people moving past for me to ever remember their faces, to clearly discern more than one in a hundred. Still twice this week I have seen the same man who looks at me as if he knows me when he doesn't. Both times, we have noticed each other from a small distance among hundreds of others riding bikes and jogging. We have each walked slowly as a piece of thread unraveling from a blanket compared to the speeding throng around us. Being strangers, we haven't stopped or spoken.

Both times I saw him, he was carrying something upon his shoulder, a large package wrapped in paper or plastic. His right arm was folded around it while his eyes danced and made conversation. Among the thousands of other limbs blurring into the skyline behind them, his expression made me aware of a beauty I walk in even while feeling far from a beautiful woman. I believe I saw him alone distinctly less because he was walking—not biking or jogging—than because he met a need I had almost forgotten. For the first time in almost too long to remember, I felt I have moved slowly underwater rather than hurried for a reason. His whole face as well as his eyes were open.

When my mom first confessed she had signed me up for the swim team, she said it was only a suggestion. I could quit whenever I wanted. It was only her way, I realized even then, of helping me lose the weight collecting on my waist, my thighs, my buttocks when I stayed sitting. If she hadn't, a decade of my life, from eight to eighteen, would have been so much drier, my skin smelling only rarely of chlorine. I joined the team then kept swimming even after I grew less rounded. I kicked my legs through liquid, indulged my one true instinct, searching for beauty hidden beneath water's surface. Once practice was finished, I took off my plastic swim cap and let my hair hang ragged.

I was never in any hurry despite my coaches' insistence on speed, always more even for those who were winning. I was never eager to leave the water's reassuring silence so long as all races ended at the beginning. Even the fastest among us swam only from one side of the pool and back again, never arrived anyplace different. I had no hunger for medals, for ribbons. I never minded losing but accepted last as my natural place. Over time, my coaches ignored me.

My mom was surprised I stayed on the team for as many years as I did, through more meets than she ever wanted to attend on weekday evenings when she could have been weeding her flower beds or doing laundry. After so many hours spent sitting through the school day, however, I began to crave the movement. It is the same reason I walk along the lakefront at workday's end for as long as the weather allows. I walk as slowly as I once swam from one side of the pool and back again while everyone else is biking or jogging except for the man who carries the package.

Weeks have passed now since I've seen him. To have recognized his face and have had his eyes twice make conversation was enough of a gift, one he has likely forgotten. Men may look upon me as a body that suffices every now and then. But judging by his expression, he saw a woman in her later thirties who could still be in the process of becoming when she walks this close to this large a body of water. As we came closer, the stars in his pupils seemed to ask a question. If he was wondering if this body is the end, as I think he might have been, I answered him simply. All lasting beauty is fluid.

The last time I saw him, the ends of my hair were wet. I was walking home from a party at a friend's apartment, where I had not yet met many of the others invited until that evening. Most were artists, and several sell their paintings for a living. The most statuesque of the women often models for the rest, she told me.

After we had talked and drunk a little wine and eaten, we swam in the pool in the building's basement. At first, I made excuses, tried leaving early. All the other women wore bikinis beneath their dresses. I had brought no swimsuit but wore my friend's one-piece when she insisted. I changed in her bedroom then followed the rest to the basement, where they stayed laughing in the shallow end as I dove into the deep end like a dolphin. While they held each other's bodies grown weightless, carrying each other on their backs like slack papooses, I swam back and forth then back and forth again. I felt at ease as long as I stayed in motion.

Later upstairs, we drank more wine while dripping water onto the floor in the kitchen, while letting our towels hang loose around our waists, our hips. The artists then drifted into the living room, leaving watery footprints. They let their swimsuits fall onto the carpet before hanging them off the balcony to dry while wearing towels only. These nine or ten men and women paid little attention to their own bodies. They walked casually back inside and changed into their clothes, which lay scattered across chairs and couches. I padded inside the bedroom to put my own clothes on again when a man opened the door without knocking. He said he was looking for his girlfriend, not seeming to notice I was wearing only panties.

The body tells each person who sees it only one story. It tells of where beauty lives and where it goes missing. Its contours, its proportions speak of strength and suppleness, of the time remaining until it turns entirely to stone, until it evolves from wetness into dryness. Seeing the man carrying his package along Lake Michigan less than an hour after this, I wondered what I told him while keeping silent.

Not long after they stop nursing, Moken children abandon their wooden boats, which are all they know of houses. They step into the sea. At an age when most Western children are still considered helpless, Moken begin to hunt and feed themselves. Their boats, or kabangs, are said to represent the human form. According to ancient legend, the boat's front forms a mouth in need of constant nourishment, the boat's back an anus. After leaving their kabang, the Moken are in some sense freed of their bodies. Weightless, with their stories forgotten, they hold their breath and meet their own private gods and goddesses.

At the public pool where I worked as a lifeguard for three summers, there were never any lives to save, none while I was working. Minimum wage was all I received in exchange for all my years on a swim team. My thousands of hours spent running through water, from one end of the pool and back again, had come to nothing, as I knew they would from the beginning. I only ever left my chair and dove into the pool to reassure those children starting to dogpaddle a little breathlessly. I had only to wrap one soft arm around their waist to comfort them as I scalloped my other through the water with an ease that surprised me. I climbed out using the ladder and, for a few minutes until my skin turned dry again, felt myself bathed in the goddess's beauty. No one else, I knew, could see this, though being seen had never been her purpose. Otherwise, she would have shown herself to me long before then.

Female lifeguards where no one is ever in danger of drowning do little more than uphold a temple built for a goddess they don't believe in. They wear whistles around their necks they rarely bother blowing. Bronzing their lean legs in the sun, they rest on wooden chairs to see everything below them and are themselves more clearly seen as a consequence. The male lifeguards spent more time in the bathhouse than we did, more hours on the intercom making announcements, sitting in the shade of the awning of the hot dog stand reading magazines. They sat in the small office playing music. They watched us. They made us feel either wanted or unwanted as the children splashed below us.

I was likely the only female lifeguard who was still a virgin. For much of those summers, I sat trying to pretend there are joys available only to the sexless. I tried making my isolation into a religion, tried telling myself something beyond what my body had already written, the only story to which most people will listen. I imagined I saw more than others around me, as if I were a Moken hunting underwater when in truth I was the opposite. I needed prescription sunglasses, had fuzzy underwater vision.

For years, my parents owned a speedboat with another family. On Sundays when I wasn't working, I usually went waterskiing, spent hours sitting on a cracked leather seat with my legs extended toward the engine and inhaled the leaking gasoline my parents complained was getting more expensive. Though skiing was their only real leisure activity, my parents often avoided the water once they found themselves surrounded by its silence. After my dad slowed the boat to where the lake was deepest, they both became reluctant to dive in. Neither liked to swim or ever spent much time in water shallow enough not to need a life jacket. As they grew older, they often said they preferred to sit and ride instead, enjoying the boat's speed while others skied behind it.

They usually relied on me to go first, and I almost always obliged them, even though I never had any love for being dragged behind our boat while struggling among rocky waves to keep my balance, feeling my arms being torn and lengthened after I finished. My lackluster feelings for doing anything in water except swim too slowly to win any races was something I knew disappointed them. Once I was old enough to drive myself to my own swim meets, they mostly stopped going.

One of the last times we went skiing while I was still working as a lifeguard, my mom hadn't worn a swimsuit. She normally wore hers beneath a summer dress, but today she planned on changing into it at the marina's rest area, as she announced to us before leaving. Only she had forgotten it at home, she said when her turn to ski came. She looked only half disenchanted with staying dry instead. This was her way, I suspected, of escaping the fun she had long tired of having.

Two of my dad's friends, both with sagging mustaches, were with us that day. As they sat drinking Pabst Blue Ribbon, they told my mom a bra and underwear were the same as a bikini. They laughed and repeated it. As they took their own turns skiing, she drank a few beers to match them. They goaded her, and eventually she did as they wanted. She had worn silk panties and a fawn lace bra beneath her dress. She had also lived more than four decades inside an attractive body. She had nothing to hide from them except a larger show of beauty.

As she handed my dad her dress, he sat facing the opposite direction. I turned and watched him study a family of ducks trace a shifting island of seaweed as he sank beer cans, one after another, while watching the ducks drift toward the horizon. Before filling each can with water until it bubbled and fell to lake's bottom, he tore off their tabs and dropped them inside a cup holder.

As my mom rose from out of the water and became a smaller person from a distance, only the dark patch of curling hair between her legs looked a different color from the rest of her. The smell of gasoline began receding as she jumped wakes in her panties. Her skin bled into the cloudless sky behind her. I wound my towel more tightly around me as the boat gathered speed and the wind kept rising. My dad's two friends howled with laughter as my dad stared straight ahead, driving us in a loose ellipse until our boat became a planet lapsed from orbit.

Centuries before this, when all the world still believed in gods and goddesses, lifeguards too may have seen as clearly underwater as dolphins. Only they had no need then to save any children from drowning. We were all drowned already. We all lived beneath the ocean. We lived out our lives swimming without hurry, bathed in beauty. To exist solely now on land is to live always waiting to reenter the water—to feel soothed even by the sound of it falling. To live a life nothing like the Moken is to feel the loss of our former lives within our very eyelids, to retain a portion of a third for no evolutionary reason. To spend nine months submerged in a womb's amniotic water is to emerge from our mothers crying, aghast at this world's desiccation.

Before our ancestors crawled out from a primordial liquid, a translucent membrane slid across the eye and moistened the lens, allowing them to see better through the blue depths of the ocean. We have inherited only its vestige. Every human who inhabits this planet retains its remnant, positioned at the eye's corner closest to the nose's bridge. Among fish, reptiles, and amphibians, the eyelid still slides horizontally across the entire eye's surface. Whereas with our own third eyelid receded into nearly nothing, with my poor underwater vision, its only purpose is to remind us we once spent more time in water than we do at present. It reminds us the last of the Sea Gypsies have all but vanished.

The ability to see as well underwater as dolphins leaves even the Moken in time, normally by their early twenties. Afterward, their eye muscles stiffen. By then, most have produced offspring, their work from nature's perspective completed. Still they stand tall in their kabangs. From this vantage, they thrust harpoons into the sea rather than fish with their hands. The light reflecting off the waves' crests at midday blinds them. They turn their heads from the water's reflection toward the high-rises overspreading nearby islands.

Some evenings, those of us who worked until pool's closing carpooled to a smaller town to eat fried chicken. After we had locked the gates, swam some ourselves, and drank beer around the hot dog stand bought by one of the lifeguard's older brothers, we drove along the highway. The ends of our hair were often wet as we ate chicken an hour or so later, though I cannot remember how many of these evenings we may have had, how often we planned them, as I can clearly remember only one of them. I rode to eat fried chicken in another lifeguard's minivan, where I sat by myself in the seat farthest from the driver.

The lifeguard seated in front of me must have been drunk or close to it, while I had been drinking nothing but water. As he started talking to me, he leaned back then wrapped his arms around my upper body. Before I could stop him, he heaved himself over the back of his seat and sat too close beside me. For the first time in my life, I felt a hardened penis. I felt him thrusting, trying to dry hump me while everyone else in the minivan was watching, laughing. I felt myself grow warm with all I had been missing, the strange abrasion women looking closer to goddesses easily attracted. I laughed then pushed him off me. I still don't know whether he was only making fun of me, half performing the sex I had never experienced. This has always been my assumption.

The next day, a note was taped to my bathhouse locker. Unsigned and scrawled in marker, it read, "I love you always." I thought the boy who dry humped me had written it, and I was hurt by the irony of its message. Later in the day, I found out a female lifeguard who was friendly toward me had done this instead. She had seen my face while the other lifeguard was rubbing himself against me. She told me as we cleaned the bathhouse floor together she understood what I was feeling. She had begun to hate this job for all the male lifeguards' comments. She thought she understood me, but she didn't. Her body told a different story.

If I were to visit this pool again, I imagine I would find the same lifeguards still presiding over the same blanket of water, still with no lives in need of saving. I cannot imagine anything real has changed. Those sitting in the same chairs at summer's end perform the same function as those I knew once did, myself included. They sit and act as columns for a temple to a goddess of whom they know nothing. When your world has yet to begin evolving into dryness, when your body tells a story that elicits love without limits, the goddess is unnecessary. For me, she was a source of beauty no one else could judge as they could my face, my body.

However pleasing or unpleasing my appearance, she promised something beyond this, a liquid essence. She continues to allow me to perceive beauty beyond the senses, which I still believe to be more vital than becoming a beautiful object. I have been too long acquainted with life's disappointments not to need this one illusion. I know the man carrying the package may not have seen me as clearly as I thought he did. I can also never know what he carried on his shoulder, only that he held it close to him. We walked slowly, passed each other as the light fell behind the buildings.

MALE NIPPLES

NURTURING INSTINCTS

There had been an accident on the highway, though no one seemed too worried. Traffic stalled, and the car doors behind us flew open. Teenage boys in sleeveless shirts started playing hacky sack along the median. Their knees, their ankles swiveled. Jeans sagged from hip bones as hair straggled free from armpits, catching the wind in places. Policemen rode past on motorcycles while reflecting the boys' serpentine movements through the mirrors of their sunglasses. I rolled down my window, and the air stopped shifting, staying stagnant. We sat there for more than two hours, until the broken cars and motorcycle were separated, their drivers taken away in ambulances to Florence.

Dozens more cars froze behind us. A phalanx of men left their engines running to walk closer to where two cars and a motorcyclist collided, a mile or more in the distance. Cigarette smoke lengthened out Roman noses as the men arched their backs and surrendered to the day's altered rhythm. Only minutes before this, most had been driving twenty miles an hour past the speed limit. Now they followed the sirens. They carried themselves like gladiators as the promise of bloodletting called them forward.

I'd been married a little less than a week then. My husband and I were both sleepless for going on twenty-four hours. The day's swelter deepened as I watched a parade of male bodies but missed their chiseled faces. My husband closed his eyes, and I noticed how Italian men wore their pants tighter, closer to their buttocks. My husband wore his own pants baggy, said he needed room for his wallet, though he never had much money and was thinner than average. I sank lower in my seat and started rotating my wedding ring around the bulb of my finger, pushing its diamond so it faced my palm instead. By the time traffic moved again, my body felt heavy with a lifetime of marriage.

When we drove into Montisi, a town of only a couple hundred residents, Roberto was waiting outside to show us where to park and take our luggage. The only other people staying at the inn were two hot-air balloon pilots from Oregon, middle-aged women undergoing divorces, something they confided to us next morning at breakfast as we sat two tables away from them. Stepping out of the car, I watched a cat stalk a lizard near the doorway of the bakery across the alley. The cat lashed its tongue toward the tail in a single, fluid movement. It devoured the living lizard with an insouciance I envied.

The cat's belly sank, sated. Roberto followed my gaze and nodded. He said cats were wonderful creatures so long as they weren't domesticated. Long as it had been since I'd had anything to do with wildness, I stretched my arms out and nodded in the lazing cat's direction. I watched its rib cage expand then contract again and widen. In my sleepless exhaustion—in my heightened or lowered awareness—I ached with the loss of the cat's same daily carnage. In one of my life's most clarifying moments, I felt I suddenly understood the underlying reason for all the world's antic violence. Our natural bloodthirst forced to atrophy, our lives gentler than the species that leads them, we inflict violence en masse with less conscience. None of the men smoking cigarettes as they walked along the highway had gone to help the accident's victims. They had gone only to inspect the mangled cars, the more mangled limbs. They had gone to confirm what happens when the normal boundaries of traffic are broken.

Less than a week before this, the Monday after my wedding, I'd returned to work and cowered at the quiet congratulations. I made my co-workers empty promises to show them pictures. Twelve years later, and I still don't have any. I have lost the few prints of what there are no digital records of to my knowledge, and I cannot say I mind this. I went through the Catholic motions only to please my parents. I decided against being either especially miserable or happy, avoiding all arguments about ceremonies, about religion. When my mom said my nurturing instincts would kick in once I confessed to her I never wanted children, I had nodded, knowing they wouldn't.

After only a few days in Italy, I finally admitted to myself how poorly I fit into my own life at the moment. Among the crooked Tuscan buildings, the wild cats and dusty bottles of chianti, I came alive to another instinct. To live a life of the senses, I only began glimpsing, is to succumb to their desire for excess. During sex, I started biting my husband's nipples, the skin smoothing his knees, his shoulder blades. I clawed at his lower back a bit, made small growling noises. Back in Chicago, we showed each other our teeth marks, our scratches. We laughed then agreed that to keep doing this might lead to darker places. We agreed, though part of me wanted to keep biting. We agreed because I knew it would have done little good explaining that for as long as I had been a girl growing into a woman, which was twenty-five years then, I had never been allowed to hurt anything. For all those who nurture things, there must be counterbalancing forces. I was starting to realize I was one of them at bottom.

In our honeymoon suite, a narrow pane of glass was cut just above the shower to let the light in. A red cord hung from the ceiling and dangled beside the toilet. A government regulation, Roberto said when he followed where my eyes went. Pull it and we'd summon emergency services. A couple weeks before this inside my studio apartment, before my husband and I moved into a larger place together, I had slipped getting out of the shower. Only half awake, I'd gotten dizzy, lost my balance. I'd cracked my head on the side of the tub then lay on the floor wet and naked. I offered my boss no explanation for coming in an hour later than expected, knowing she wouldn't want to hear the reason, knowing the reason too was stupid. Italians, though, had foreseen how easily this might happen. I could have come here alone and been as safe as I was with my husband. In Montisi, the bruises on my knees were turning from blue to yellowish.

Roberto left our room, my husband lay down on the bed, and I showered in the stare of the sun. The window above my head, I realized, was a person. No wider than my body, the window could accommodate only the smallest portion of the sky's vastness, allowing only one cloud at a time in. Unable to control the shape of each one drifting past, however dark or flocculent, the pane of glass was only a witness. It could never have existed and nothing would have been any different. The window indulged none of its own destructive urges. For any rain to pour in, someone else would have to break it.

This was my life now, I said to myself as my hair began to smell of the shampoo's citrus, its shards of squeezed oranges. My husband started snoring as I rinsed my hair, as I half deluded myself into thinking this was real life, not a vacation. Still for a week, I told myself this was life as it should be. Should I fall in the shower while my husband was sleeping, Italian men wearing their pants tighter than Americans would come and rescue me. Accidents here were taken more easily for granted. Even on the highway, the sirens sounded a more muted panic. While hundreds of men had walked up to examine the carnage, the women they left behind them lounged on car trunks, elongated smooth necks with closed eyelids. They shook their sandals off so their feet hung lank over the highway's cement carpet. Only the Americans had stayed seated inside their cars with their seatbelts fastened.

From the window's height above the shower, the ceiling angled so much lower toward the bed that the room looked made for two species of humans, one only half the size of the other. Each morning, I rapped my head against the beam above where I slept while my taller husband managed to avoid this. When my eyes watered with fresh pain and I flopped my head back on my pillow again, he offered me less sympathy than I wanted. I closed my eyes as he showered, as he enjoyed his own time with the window who was a person. While the water fell below the square of sky, sibilant and soothing, I listened to the hot-air balloon pilots two floors below us talking to Roberto, who was offering them pastries from the bakery across the alley. The inn's walls were thin, and I wondered if they had heard me hit my head again, if Roberto too had shuddered. If we had any other room besides the honeymoon suite, this would not have happened.

I no longer remember when Roberto told us he had gotten his own divorce only a couple months before this. He may have never told me directly. Looking back, I realize he probably didn't. Otherwise, I feel certain the memory would come clear again. He likely confided this only to my husband, telling him in private how he had left Rome and tried starting his life over, had tried but was maybe failing. I only know when I saw Roberto after I knew this, when he waited up to make sure we arrived safely back from a long drive to Umbria, this seemed obvious. The skin below his eyes looked heavy, though it may have only been fatigue, too many late nights, too many early mornings. The signs may have been there all along without me noticing. He wore the same yellow cotton sweater three days in a row, something I can still see clearly. His nipples poked through the fabric. I saw suggestions of the small breasts men sometimes grow with aging, hinting they have become more feminine, more nurturing. Life here, I thought, had a softness to match the landscape. If Roberto was suffering, he was doing so beautifully.

Our last full day in Tuscany, Roberto left for Rome to visit his mother, who lived alone, elderly and with all her teeth, he boasted. He would be gone until late evening, so he gave us the key to the front door, asking us to lock it before we went to bed. His wide eyebrows were combed back toward his forehead. His loafers smelled of polish, of sweetened almonds. Although temperatures had climbed into the upper eighties, he wore a tweed jacket with velvet elbow patches. Before we left the next morning, we gave him a bottle of wine and a blue hydrangea we bought in a town where we had eaten dinner then watched a wedding procession fill the piazza with singing, with pale and yellow roses, on what might have been our last night in this part of Italy for the rest of our lives but wasn't. Roberto said he would save the wine until we returned, for the three of us to share, in the afternoon if we wanted. We signed the guest book of the Locanda di Montisi. We waved then left Roberto alone to clean all the cups we had dirtied.

Five years later, I made our second reservation through the inn's online booking system. I didn't send Roberto a message. He had likely forgotten us, I reasoned. He might have moved back to Rome again, having exhausted Tuscany's quiet. During one of our last conversations at breakfast, he mentioned he had been skiing four years ago in Colorado with his ex-wife and some friends. He wanted to visit the West again, he confided. He wanted to buy a cowboy hat, to learn to wrangle a bull if we could promise to show him. We told him we would meet him anywhere he wanted. Yet apart from the mass Christmas and Easter emails he sent to all his former guests, we never heard from him.

Inside the Locanda's intimate front office, still papered with medieval maps crumpled at their edges, Roberto was absent. I tapped the same silver bell still resting on the desk now losing its varnish when a woman with a wandering green eye rushed inside to greet us. Her dark hair was wriggling loose from a braid, which was falling down her back into a second spinal column. Her external coccyx was fraying and uneven. It had been too long since she cut her hair. The ends were splitting into factions.

She introduced herself as Mariella and confessed our room wasn't ready yet as I tried to still my focus, to look into only the eye that held me steady. There were no other guests, we noticed next morning, when the cup for my coffee betrayed remnants of lipstick from another woman. When we asked for Roberto as she confirmed our reservation, she said he had left the inn a couple years ago to open his own taverna, bringing the town's number of restaurants to two, doubling them. We asked where it was, and she said down a few doorsteps. She threw her arm sideways and pointed. We could eat dinner there while waiting for her to clean our room if we wanted.

Reaching the taverna, we found a wooden sign slung over the gate to the patio saying both in English and Italian that the restaurant would not open before seven. Almost as tired from our flight and drive as we'd been five years before this, we slept for an hour in an olive grove sloping gently toward a flatter surface. For pillows, we bundled our jackets, while the day's lingering warmth ensured no need for blankets. Walking back again once the sun started falling behind hills growing plusher as they receded in the distance, we heard English-speaking voices filling the air above several place settings now laid in slim, symmetrical precision. They came from what appeared to be a large, extended family discussing varietals of honey. They sounded like Americans from somewhere around Boston. I couldn't see any honey, however, on any of the four tables Roberto had placed together for them.

That evening and for every evening we ate there afterward, Roberto was the taverna's only server. He had hired a chef but later acknowledged he didn't trust him. He ended up cooking most of the meals himself, he said, wasting the wages he paid him. With his American guests, we noticed he was kind and patient, though he refused to serve them any wine until after the meal was well in progress, after the primi piatti were already eaten. He liked, his said, his establishment quiet, while my husband and I stood outside the gate, hushed and expectant. Whether he would remember us, we were both uncertain.

Both the taverna and the inn had inevitably seen thousands of versions of us, Americans sleeping late and speaking poor Italian, since we left. When I creaked the gate open, Roberto's eyes sparkled, though, widened. He approached me with his arms outstretched. He hugged me for several seconds then shook hands with my husband. He said he had drunk the wine we gave him but planted the hydrangea. He left his other guests and showed us to the taverna's garden, where he grew herbs, white asparagus, edible flowers to accent his dishes. The hydrangea had lost then never regained any of its blue blossoms, he admitted. I felt grateful he kept our gift yet also disappointed at its inability to flower again.

We turned back toward the kitchen. A woman with cropped hair dyed cinnamon approached us and smiled as if we knew her when we didn't. Her blue eyes blazed electric, and she spoke with a honeyed Southern accent. She wore her own pants fitted tightly to her buttocks as if she were male, Italian. She wore so dark a color of lipstick, so many silver bracelets weighting lean and freckled wrists, that I felt embarrassed, too conscious of the beauty she had lost years ago. I felt she had still not come to terms with this. The first three buttons of her blouse were undone, revealing wrinkled cleavage. She also seemed at ease inside her body, whose movements had a smoothness, a languor to them. Roberto wrapped his arm around her shoulders and told us Gail was from Georgia. He said this then repeated it, I think, because neither my husband nor I reacted.

She stretched her arm low across his hips then slipped her hand inside his back pocket. I felt certain they had sex more than people of their age normally managed, more than myself and my husband. Though twenty years younger, I sensed Gail was stronger than I could ever be or ever had been. She seated us at a table farthest from the entrance. She handed us our menus, paper coated in plastic, as I inhaled some of her vanilla perfume and noticed her fingernails were sharpened into daggers. I watched her sway back inside the kitchen, watched Roberto's eyes follow her, and saw the power she wielded over a man I realized I had liked a little sadder. Yet Gail was the cat, Roberto the lizard. Unlike most of us, they seemed one with nature.

I looked at them and remembered being a girl in rural Indiana, probably not yet in kindergarten, and leaving my parents on the porch swing as I ran to chase a black kitten, one of dozens of feral ones then roaming our garden. I caught the cat by the tail and showed my parents, who both told me to hold it gently. My dad said not to dangle a living thing as if it were dead already, when I felt some of the shame he intended. I curled the kitten's spine into a roundness, contracted my own body, and held the mewling animal as if it were a baby. I rocked the kitten until it started crying so loudly I hated the sound of it.

The cat clawed my cheek, left it bleeding, and I swung it by its tail again. I swung the animal in punishment, my mom and dad scolded me once more, until I dropped it on the grass then watched it vanish into the shadows of our rhubarb patches. I have never willingly held a cat since then. I left them alone, became allergic. My husband, I knew, would have liked one in our Chicago apartment, but I didn't want to always be taking medication. Since my parents both died so much younger than expected, since both grew sick soon after my husband and I returned from Montisi, I didn't want to have to care for anything weaker than I was already. I knew there would only be the same temptation to hurt it again, and I had already seen how well cats fared on their own in Italy.

In Roberto's taverna, on the patio where all his tables were set, I sat facing the buildings across the street, where children were playing soccer, dodging only occasional traffic. Gail came back from the kitchen and asked if she could sit beside us, get to know us better. She wanted to take my seat, however. She told me to sit level with the last of the sun, which still was setting. She turned my chair facing west while she became an avian silhouette stripped of its plumage, so thin were her limbs for an older woman. She allowed herself to watch lizards race down drainpipes, cats slurp them with indifference, while I saw only sunspots. She said I should never miss a Tuscan sunset, though I was blinded all the same. There was still too much light for me to see that which was disappearing.

I raised my hand for shade when she asked me to take it down again so we could see each other's faces. She said the sun would set soon enough, too quickly. Still it hovered orange and ripe and rotting for longer than she promised, from the bruschetta to the panna cotta, which Roberto said he made from a family recipe. Before we left that evening, Gail took a picture of us sitting beside each other, my husband's arm hung loosely over my shoulder while I squinted into the camera, whose flash double blinded me. In what she emailed me a few weeks later, my pink bra strap lay exposed and slanted on the shoulder my husband was hugging. My eyes were almost closed. This was the way she and Roberto would have to remember me, however, should they be the type of people to organize their photos into albums. Our own pictures from our two trips to Montisi must be somewhere, though where don't ask me.

Roberto wore an apron for much of the last time we saw him, for what I now feel safer saying is probably forever. Still we could tell he had lost some weight, was maybe fifteen pounds thinner. He wore no yellow sweater this time through which I could see his nipples sagging. In Gail's presence, his small breasts receded. He became more masculine, more assertive, refusing to serve his customers wine until the meal was halfway finished. My husband thought his face had more color than the time before this. Our old innkeeper looked five years younger rather than five years older. The first time we met, though, I saw nothing wrong with him.

For my life to fit me better, I see now more clearly than I wish, I had to lose my parents not long after we first flew back from Florence, when the memories were still too fresh for me to think of making another visit. My life had to break me into a thousand pieces for me to breathe more freely inside its limits. After their deaths, I still had a job that held little personal meaning, still only editing other people's writing. I still was married to the same man, still living in the same city. I had no real desire to change these things. Yet I felt newly free to inflict a certain daily carnage, and this has made all the difference. I became a slightly feral thing, used coarser language, wore tighter clothing, screamed more loudly during arguments with my husband, occasionally still bit him. No more Catholic ceremonies, no more talk of grandchildren. No more naturalizing of female nurturing instincts when men are equally capable of growing breasts with weight gain, with aging. I never asked Gail if she had any children, but I suspect, I hope, she didn't. Her destructive instinct seemed too well-developed. Roberto reaped the benefits.

The morning we left Montisi, Roberto met us in the bakery for coffee. Encouraged by his wondering aloud when we'd come back again, I asked whether he loved Gail when they first met, however that happened. Laughing from his abdomen, he asked, But didn't she tell you the story? At dinner the evening you met while I was in the kitchen? I shrugged, confessed she didn't. Roberto leaned back farther in his seat and said during her visit with her ex-husband, a couple years before this, she made advances. While her husband was napping, she pressed Roberto into a linen closet. Her mouth watered as she rubbed herself against him. My own mouth fell a little open, and Roberto waved his hand, said he never even considered it. He had turned his face from her lips, called her a wild woman. He opened the door of the closet and went about his business.

A couple months after she flew back to Georgia with her husband, Gail received the same Christmas email sent to all his former guests. She interpreted it as personal and earnest. She filed for divorce in Atlanta within a month then booked her trip back across the ocean, a one-way ticket. I received the same emails as she did, I told Roberto, laughing. I took them all to mean nothing, and he nodded. When I read the first one, my parents both were dying, I didn't mention to him. Unlike Gail, I had no need to kill anything. I had no need to use my woman's strength to hurt my husband, my marriage, as I now see could have happened. Life had done the killing for me.

We left Roberto and Gail for another part of Italy, closer to the Adriatic, where we swam with a man who looked like Napoleon and I sculled my hands at water's surface for hours as the sun was setting, as I looked across the water in the opposite direction. I performed fellatio on my husband on top of a stone tower dating back to the ancient Romans with seagulls screeching overhead, with footsteps of other tourists sounding in the closing distance. Gail assured us we would enjoy our time there, and I had no reason to doubt anything she said. Although she didn't have an Italian visa, although she had to travel frequently back to Atlanta because Roberto was wary of another marriage, in the past few years she'd still managed to see almost all the country. She and Roberto were planning a trip there themselves come autumn.

Roberto waved while growing smaller in our rearview mirror as the dust gradually obscured him completely. When he'd casually spoken of his mother still living in Rome, still with all her teeth as we chewed our pastries, I had wanted him to know I was changed forever since last seeing him. I wanted to tell him that my eyes stung so much in the light now I often left my apartment only after dusk on weekends. I wanted to say that Gail did her best to blind me by making me stare into the sunset. I wanted to see if I could elicit his sympathy. There was never time, however. From his perspective, we were the same couple we had been. Now his life had room for only for happiness, of which we wished him and Gail a lifetime and left him.

PALMARIS LONGUS

THE END OF LONGING

After my husband left for work this morning, I made another cup of coffee and washed dishes. I wiped soapy hands across jeans before lifting my shirt up to a mirror that we lean against a window ledge in our kitchen. Where glass rests against more glass, I looked into the smaller rectangle and saw fresh evidence of the fact I've lost a little weight over the summer. My waist and stomach have shrunken, though my husband hasn't noticed. While he goes to work in a downtown Chicago office and I work from our apartment, an egg inside my ribs keeps expanding and presses on my diaphragm. Early mornings when I first awaken, I sense the sheen of its unbornness. Falling back asleep, I watch myself give birth not to a baby but to myself again. I tell myself I'll have another lifetime for everything I've always wanted. I tell myself I can afford to do little more in this one than watch life happen.

One Friday evening in Manhattan, where my husband and I were spending a weekend a couple of weeks before this, we had a rare evening of fullness. The evening left us with nothing that either of us still wanted. Two of my closest friends and their spouses met us for dinner in the West Village, where we stayed for hours talking after our food was finished. None of us were in a hurry to leave our wholeness, to begin breaking it into pieces. Near eleven, an actor best known for a TV series that ended more than a decade ago walked into our corner of the courtyard. The play he was starring in had finished production. He sat at the table across from us beneath a garland of paper lanterns, and he seemed to be at ease so long as we kept ourselves from staring.

Earlier that evening, before we had met our friends, my husband and I walked past the theater where he was performing. We saw his face and the play's title, *The End of Longing*, without wanting to buy tickets, without even giving it consideration. Since his TV series aired its last season, the actor has become better known for his alcohol and drug addiction. Less attractive in person than I would have expected, he drank water only and sat at the far end of the table from his castmates, who ordered wine, beer, and salads. His smile stayed toothless while they were laughing.

Unlike many of my friends and unlike my husband, I have never wanted to live in New York City. I have never wanted to move somewhere that leads more easily than other places to dreams of living an alternative existence. I have never wanted to pay more money for a smaller apartment, to ride more crowded subways than Chicago has already, to pursue another direction than my life has taken. Yet the morning after our evening of fullness, I could not help wishing some things were different. I could not help wishing my eyes were blue and sparkling rather than dull and brown. My last morning in this city for what I imagine will be a long time to come had started with my husband staring into my face as my eyes blinked open. Gazing at me with concern and revulsion, he told me to look in the mirror, when he watched me face my own reflection and absorb the fact my right eye was bleeding.

An internet search confirmed my symptoms matched those of a subconjunctival hemorrhage. Though frightening to witness, the condition is not serious. This form of internal bleeding is normally caused by too hard of sneezing, coughing, or straining from constipation. In the past few days, however, I had done none of these things. Overnight, after the evening of fullness ended, some blood vessels had simply burst at random. New York City is also one that can easily cause blood to break open from arteries. It can easily delude things into breaching their natural boundaries.

After we dressed and walked to Chelsea to buy breakfast, my eye was still weeks away from healing. Already forgetting the strain New York put on my body, my husband said he would never return to the Midwest again if he had his way about things. Temperatures had reached the mid-nineties as we bought bagels and iced coffee, as I continued walking several steps behind him. The air stank of sidewalk garbage, though my husband claimed he couldn't smell it. Where I saw pools of urine, he only stretched his neck higher toward the tops of the buildings.

As we wandered closer toward the Village, an apartment complex with a striking art deco entrance caught his attention. He stopped and told me to look at what I knew had been a boutique hotel only a couple of years before this. When he pointed to the lapidary beauty of its cornices, I nodded in silence. I let him think he was the first one of us to see this. He would have had no way of knowing I stayed here once before without him, though he would have remembered me leaving him for the weekend had I taken time to remind him. He would have remembered having wanted to go with me when I told him I wanted to spend time with my friends without him. At the time, he seemed to understand this. He also did not ask me where I was staying, because he assumed I was staying with my friend who lives in Harlem.

I never told him that one of the friends I was visiting lives in Chicago, not New York City. Almost ten years older than I am, Sara lives only a matter of blocks away from our own apartment building. She has been married for decades to someone I have always found funny and handsome. Still she asked me if I wanted to meet her in Manhattan along with another man she was sleeping with. She asked me if I wanted to watch her live out an alternative existence. Looking back, I can see she must have known what my answer would be even before I did. Otherwise, she would hardly have risked telling me about the affair she was having. She must have sensed a desire for another life stirring inside me even if she knew nothing about the egg weighing on my diaphragm, pressing as it grows against my sternum. Had she ever really known me, had she ever seen me clearly, she would have understood I am content with waiting, with doing little more than watching.

At the time, I often met her for coffee at a bakery halfway between our two buildings. Sometimes I arrived early to engage in the briefest of interactions with its manager, whom I found attractive and often kept me sane during days of petty conflict with my husband. His dark and curling hair, the length of his eyelashes, the smoothness of his movements as he reached for a scone or muffin made my own life seem less random. Sometimes I lingered at his counter shamelessly. I wanted nothing in these moments beyond prolonging a relationship best characterized by being completely painless. Inevitably, I gained a little weight in the process, consuming more pastries than I needed. There is always a price to pay, though, for passing pleasure that amounts to nothing. I have gone there less and less since meeting Sara in New York City. Since my right eye was bloodied, I have no intention of ever returning. I am done with longing.

After I told her yes, I would meet her for the weekend, Sara confessed that she and her lover see each other in Chicago fairly often. In New York, however, they could be freer of their spouses. They could love each other in public, could roll over on top of each other in Central Park near one of its oldest stone bridges. Had the manager of the bakery paid her the same amount of attention as he paid to me, Sara said she would have taken it further. Had they had any chemistry, had her light not already dispersed itself among so many other men already, she would have seduced him. As it was, she said she found him too skinny, a comment I suspected was voiced from defensiveness because she felt ignored by him, because with her he rarely made eye contact. I knew she wanted me to ask her questions, allowing her space to tout her sexual successes. Instead, I changed the subject.

When I first walked inside the lobby of the Midtown hotel where Sara and her lover were staying, I had been curious, expectant. I wanted to see someone I knew fairly well inhabit another life in another city. I sat waiting for them for twenty or more minutes. On one of the lobby's velvet couches, I could have opened the book I kept inside my purse and had been reading on the plane. I kept my purse zipped, however. I looked down at my legs and then stared into my inner wrists. Thinking Sara could still be having sex at this moment, I studied my wrists' central useless tendon, which allows for no tighter grip, makes me no stronger a person. Should another tendon rupture, a surgeon could use this one to replace it. I knew this only because Sara had once told me this happened to her after a bicycle accident. This tendon had been grafted onto her thigh, helping her repair the damage. Her right inner arm had looked strangely smooth compared to her left one ever since. Then she confessed she had fallen half in love with her surgeon. She said she would have slept with him were she not heavily sedated.

Both of my own tendons still reach for my inner elbows without touching them. Each one resembles a string tied to a balloon that has floated into the sky and left me stranded. They are matching strings connecting my body to nothing beyond it. That Sara has only one left now seems almost symbolic, whereas I still have my fantasies if I need them. I still can let them go, watch them vanish. Whenever I lift my shirt up and see my stomach, I know for certain how much good going to the bakery less and less has done me. I know I was ten or more pounds heavier two years before this as I sat waiting for Sara and her lover in the lobby.

Eventually, she called and told me to come up to their room because she wasn't ready yet. She needed more time to apply her makeup, to finish her coffee. Nearly noon and she was still wearing a robe, still braless. Two empty champagne bottles lay sideways on the dresser. It had been only a few weeks since I had last seen her, yet her eyes slanted higher up at the edges than I remembered. Back in Chicago a little more than a week later, she admitted to having plastic surgery. Defending herself without me accusing her of anything, she said it wouldn't be long before I'll want to do something similar, before I'll find attracting men's attention isn't easy. I knew as I sat waiting for her to dress for our day in Manhattan that she had told herself the reason I had come here was only because I lacked courage to do what she was doing. This weekend, it was already clear she was going to have her way with everything.

When I first met the man she was sleeping with, I couldn't help but notice he was balding and chubby. Sara's husband was far more charismatic, more hirsute with a far more sculpted body. When her lover stretched his hand out to me, I grasped a palm that felt as soft as a baby's. He wore a salmon V-neck sweater and laughed at everything I said even when I wasn't being funny. He told me he had bought Sara several leopard-print blouses the night before this. They all had sequins for eyes staring out from where her nipples hung behind them. When she flew onto the floor to show me, he rhapsodized about how sexy she looked wearing each one. His worship of her, of all her vanity, I realized was his main attraction, what made him necessary. I told myself I could not imagine ever sleeping with someone who gave himself away this easily, who had such terrible taste in clothing. Had I ever been similarly tempted, had the manager of the bakery ever asked me to meet him after closing, seeing Sara with her lover might have saved me.

Once we left and started walking toward the nearest subway, neither one of them felt like visiting any of the museums Sara had said we would visit. They both wanted to do more shopping as they walked with their hands inside each other's back pockets. After a lunch of sandwiches and salads, I suggested that we separate until early evening. I told them I wanted to visit the Whitney, a special exhibition. After glancing at the gift shop, however, after seeing the price for admission, I decided instead to sit outdoors at a café. I took my book from my purse and started reading. I looked up and could not help noticing I was being noticed by a table of two men across from me. Crossing one leg over its opposite, I watched as other men in passing turned their heads toward my aloneness. I realized I could take a lover here if I wanted. I realized there was power in turning my head back to my book, power in withholding.

A group of much younger women walked past me in heels that sounded as if they might puncture the pavement. The shortest and most brightly attired was holding balloons, each one inflated into the shape of a phallus. A bachelorette party then. As the one holding the balloons moved closer to the intersection, she let go of them all, seemingly by accident. The two men at the table across from me laughed as the other bachelorettes started shrieking, only pretending to be disappointed. The balloons soon would have become annoying to carry wherever they were going. Better to have had a weak grip, I thought. Better to have lost them.

I left the café and watched the last of the balloons vanish behind clouds that had thrown them into relief. I looked toward more men turning to look at me as I kept walking and remembered how, when I was only six or seven, the Indiana sky's grayness had swallowed hundreds of other balloons, all an orangish red, all looking fire tipped from a distance. Instead of male anatomy, they had better resembled the egg that still fills my ribs to bursting. They were the shape of innocence, of pure promise. They were all inflated with helium that as children we were not allowed to inhale and in this way shorten the frequencies of our already high and bleating voices.

Attached to each one had been a library card, on the back of which was printed a handwritten name and address. There had been one balloon for each person hoping for someone else to find it across an ocean. From a parking lot facing a gas station, everyone in our Catholic school released a piece of string from their hand after counting down from ten in unison. Unlike the bachelorettes, we had done this on purpose. Until we stood waving goodbye to the hundreds of balloons as a body, I had not known we were lost, in need of saving. Yet we were now giving the sky, the balloons, a mission.

Most of my teachers were middle-aged women wearing baggy blouses. Letting go of a balloon bearing their personal information was as close as most would ever come to allowing a message of pure desire escape them. This was the 1980s, the town too small for indiscretions, online flirtations not then an option. All were also married with children. However pure their motives, they had still sent something of themselves wafting into the distance. Our lives are not good enough, they as good as told their balloons before letting them go, before risking being known to someone far and foreign. They had more than likely smiled to themselves, knowing this would never happen. However contented with lives they may have wished were different in only the smallest ways, they remained the ones who thought of this. We were only children.

Sara and her lover planned to meet me in my own hotel lobby before we had dinner and then went to see live comedy, a show for which we had bought tickets a week ago. I was waiting on the elevator when she texted that they wanted to come and see my room for a moment. I texted back there wasn't much to see, but she insisted. After I let them in, she asked me to take her picture against the window with the Freedom Tower glittering in the distance. This was the hotel she had showed online to her husband before leaving, she admitted. She told me he would know the one in Midtown, for which her lover was paying, was too expensive. She instructed me to keep the bed out of the frame, as her husband would expect to see twins, not a queen bed. In the first picture I had taken, her lover's reflection appeared in the glass behind her. Sara laughed then deleted it while telling him to stand in the bathroom instead, where he retreated, giggling. She had me take another as she smiled more widely, looked a little less genuinely happy. As I handed her phone back to her, I found myself feeling sorry for Sara's husband, someone she often claimed likely had his own dalliances. I felt used by her even though I consented. She was asking me to do more than watch life happen.

After the three of us left my hotel with the art deco entrance, we walked through the West Village. Looking for someplace to eat among dozens, I had almost forgotten Sara could be so picky. Nothing pleased her despite her claims that she was starving, and I sensed her power over her lover had made her even pickier than she would normally be. After she browsed each menu, after she stepped inside each successive entrance to examine the ambiance and seating arrangements, she left frowning. None of the endless options had anything she wanted. We bypassed all the Asian, Mediterranean, and Italian, all those with courtyard seating. The farther we walked, the less time we had before the stand-up comedy show started. Eventually we settled for gyros that we ate standing on the street corner once I told her we had time for nothing else, once all of us were famished. Sara insisted this was the real way to eat in New York City.

Inside the club, we were seated almost at the comedians' feet. Our knees rubbed the stage because we walked in only seconds before the show started, because everyone else wanted to avoid the spotlight shining partly down on them as well. The man Sara was sleeping with started laughing before anyone said anything funny, and each of the three of us in turn became the comedians' focus. Clearly visible from their vantage, we were their easiest targets. Sara was wearing one of her leopard-print blouses, and while I no longer remember what I was wearing, I know I allowed myself to look more like a woman than I often do in Chicago. Working from my apartment, sometimes going days with speaking only to my husband, I have little reason. Whatever my dress or outfit may have been that evening, Sara said it attracted attention. I know my legs, which are longer than hers though no longer than average, were showing. Beneath the glow of the stage lights, her dyed auburn hair also struck me as garish, her makeup too heavy. Despite her plastic surgery, the flesh around her chin folded when she looked down toward the high heels she was wearing. I vowed in that moment to abandon my own vanity, before I turn into an older woman who carries it around as lifeless baggage. In the two years that have passed, I have weeded many of my tighter clothes from my closet. I have weeded some but not all of them.

As I walked past the same comedy club a couple weeks ago with my husband after our evening of fullness, he asked me to take a picture of him standing in front of it. He told me it was famous, to which I nodded with my right eye bloodied behind my sunglasses. Before we had left the Midwest for this weekend, I had asked him if he wanted me to buy tickets to see a live performance, either here or somewhere else in the Village. When he told me no, I felt myself fill with disappointment. I was forced to acknowledge that part of the reason I asked him was because I wanted to see if the man at the door taking tickets, if any of the same comedians, might remember me and how I had looked in whatever I was wearing even though I knew there was no chance of this, not in this vast of a city with so many thousands of tourists. Almost on a daily basis, I try reminding myself that having someone else acknowledge your existence does not make your life more valid. Having other men notice you doesn't mean fewer spats with your husband.

Walking past the comedy club I had once been inside but he hadn't, my husband sighed and said this was life as it should be lived. He said this with his arms raised wide to the city's penthouses. He said this with some real bitterness while casting his gaze back toward the door where tonight more people would be laughing, where someone else would serve as the comedians' target. Walking into Washington Square Park, past disheveled men playing chess and smoking, my husband confessed he often feels his life is unfair to him. Because I have no desire to live here, because I prefer a quieter existence in a smaller city, he says he has no real chance at dreaming. He claims he tries not to, but sometimes he blames me for his life's limitations.

Roaming the steaming streets of Manhattan while the air smelled of urine and garbage, he said he felt alive here in a way that at home he simply didn't. Maybe he didn't know about Sara and the man she slept with, but here he felt more freedom, maybe the possibility of more exciting women, regardless. I have spent considerably less time with Sara in the two years since meeting her in New York City for the weekend. I have let our friendship fade into nearly nothing. I had almost forgotten about her until I walked past the boutique hotel that is now an apartment complex where I was forced to take her picture with the Freedom Tower in the distance. However disappointing one lover may have been, I know there have been others, have been many. Telling myself I wish only good things for her, I also comfort myself thinking how little we have in common.

In my apartment, I hold my shirt up to the mirror, look for my ribs appearing. I sense the faintest outline of an egg above my diaphragm, though I doubt I will ever give birth to anything besides myself again in this lifetime. There is also something consoling in housing so much life, silent and waiting. Something pure and whole resting deep inside my solar plexus.

The End of Longing bills itself as a play about broken people who become unbroken. Four strangers, all with various dysfunctions, meet in a bar and then help each other to find redemption. The play's star enacts a version of himself, an aging alcoholic. From the few reviews I have read, most critics have skewered the play as self-serving. The reason the main character drinks to excess stems from his feeling that he has never gotten all the love he needed. Before the play begins, another girlfriend has just left him. What he longs for beyond another female body to soothe him, to tame his restlessness, is never stated. Without having seen the play, I doubt it is the love of another person, however. The real reason I believe the play was hardly worth the price of a ticket is because he is looking for someone who serves no purpose. In this city where he lives, he cannot allow this lifetime to pass without much happening, to let his fingers loosen from strings attached to what is only another sphere of plastic filled with helium.

TONSILS

WINTER HONEY

There is only one man living, now well into his eighties, whose cattle still swim between islands for fresh grazing. Every October in Scotland's Outer Hebrides, he ushers his herd to Stenscholl Island, where they feed on cold, tough grass until spring. Once warmer weather returns, he rows beside them as their heads jut inches above water's surface. He shepherds them back to the Isle of Skye, from whose shores my husband and I once sailed out on a dinghy in hopes of spotting eagles in danger of extinction. It was late May when we visited, early in our marriage. We were wearing sweaters and jeans, with no intention ourselves of swimming. We didn't see either the man or his cattle, as it happens. At the time, we also didn't know to look out for them in the vast Sea of the Hebrides.

Our guide handed us binoculars so we could better see the eagles camouflaged against the cliffs and also glimpse the

163

surrounding puffins. I took more pleasure, though, in watching Portree's row of pastel houses recede from our boat's small wake until no more color was left dotting the horizon. Hours afterward, I loved seeing the same houses reappear even more. As we came closer to the dock, I again made out the small windows' curtains, the plants in ceramic pots framing doorways, the wooden mailboxes shaped into simple houses. I usually enjoy things more when no one draws my attention to them, however. I can better hold them inside then.

I saw these same eagles again last night on a documentary about these same islands. I saw them more clearly on TV from inside my Chicago apartment than I ever did in person. A woman wearing a yellow rain jacket interviewed this man I never spotted rowing his boat in northern Scotland, where he leads the same breed of Hereford cattle I grew up with from island to island. Only throughout my coming of age in southern Indiana, throughout my whole life until last evening, I had never known these cows could swim. The last man alive maintaining this custom said he swam along with his herd until his early seventies, and to the camera he confessed he missed this. He said swimming by way of bringing them to fresh grazing had always been such a joy to him that he didn't understand why no one else now did the same, why younger men with more energy than they knew what to do with had abandoned the practice. He said something about all the younger generation was missing. His ancestors had done so since before the birth of Christ, as his own grandfather had insisted. His muscles' weakness was all that stopped him.

To the cows themselves, however, swimming may not offer the same sense of exhilaration. For all the farmer knows, the younger generation might be sparing them unnecessary exertion as well as exposure to waters many consider glacially cold even during summer. There is no way of knowing, of asking them. Still, even cows weighing thousands of pounds grow buoyant when immersed in the sea, and they must feel this. It is hard not to imagine them enjoying the sense of their own lightness, reveling in temporary freedom from the heaviness of their bodies. Given the fact they are fed fat for slaughter, the temperature must also bother them less than it once did the farmer who herds them. In this way, the cows must benefit from their extra layers of insulation. They must enjoy becoming weightless without restricting their diet.

A few weeks ago, I flew from Chicago to southern Indiana to run through sprinklers and fall into the gentler rhythm of my sister's softer days among lusher vegetation. I went there too to celebrate my nephew's fifth birthday, to swim with him at his pool party, as I had promised. The flight takes little longer than loading the plane but is easier for me than driving, even though my sister must drive an hour to the airport to come and fetch me. For months before this, I had told my nephew on the phone over and over again how I was coming to eat lion cake with him. Each time, he roared at me and I roared back, the hungrier lion.

Leaving the airport for the highway leading back to her home where she raises bees and chickens, my sister handed me a tube of lipstick. She said it was a belated present for my birthday, for which she had sent flowers already. She knows I wear darker colors as a habit, but this was nice for summer, she told me. Applying it as she navigated traffic, I acknowledged it felt softer on my lips than the kind I wore normally. It was made from beeswax, she added. It was made from honeycomb that bees no longer need after the honey inside them has been eaten. She checked the rearview mirror after passing a station wagon and said a lighter color looked nice on me.

Strapped to his car seat behind me, my nephew asked me what I had on my teeth when I turned and smiled at him. My sister laughed and said Aunt Melissa has streaks of lipstick running across her teeth quite often, which was a revelation to me. She looked at me, absorbing my change of expression, then turned up the radio. My nephew shouted over Ryan Adams that he had a red line too on his teeth, and I knew in this way he still loved me. I knew and was relieved, perhaps more than I should have been. He has no way of knowing he is my most reliable means of determining how far I may have strayed from being someone still worth loving. In time, I expect his love to lessen. For years, it has come almost too easily. Every time I see him, I expect the lessening but am still not ready.

Seeing the geode slice that hangs as a pendant from a chain on my neck when I sat down to eat later that evening, my nephew asked if he could hold my totem, a word he has learned means something sacred from a cartoon he watches. My sister shook her head no from the kitchen, mouthing he would break it. I smiled to myself and told him I needed to wear this necklace always, something holy with a hole inside to match it. I whispered I drew power from the hole lined with crystals looking as if they could melt like snow in sun yet resist the temptation.

The next day, I stood in my sister's guest bedroom and lathered my face with sunscreen before my nephew's pool party. I slipped a cotton dress over my bathing suit and painted my lips their old darker color. When I had looked in a mirror earlier, I thought my lips were disappearing and realized I didn't want this to happen. Two of my sister's friends, beekeepers with children close to my nephew's and niece's ages, met us at the city pool for the celebration. Kind and wholesome, they brought a carton of ice cream to eat with cake made into the face of a lion.

When I asked how their hives were faring, they said fine then mentioned they had inspected my sister's beehives last weekend. They came over, at her asking, because her hives had started swarming. Most apiarists try to prevent what is no more than a natural method of colony reproduction, as fewer bees in one location means less honey. They said they'd worn no beekeeping suits, no netting to cover their faces. They had used the smoker, however, which normally suffices, then had each been stung badly. They showed me the welts along their arms and legs, saying that in all their years of beekeeping they had never received any stings this virulent. Wild bees, they called them.

After my nephew blew out his candles' flames, my sister cut me the smallest piece of cake she could manage. Over the past few years, she has noticed me avoiding calories that provide little nutrition. She has tried making allowances for my aversion toward sugar, though my private feeling is she only half approves of this. I picked at the brown cake with my fingers, leaving my fork clean. Seeing everyone else eat their own slice with ice cream in the full stare of the sun, I soon left them for a patch of shade. I sat on the ground, crossed my legs, and imagined the inside of their summer bodies packed in snow. I envisioned their red organs becoming blue and frostbitten. I imagined, half envied, their stomach, their liver, their kidneys' relief from the heat. This is what sugar has always been to me, snow mixed with flour and baked in an oven. A way of cooling something burning.

My growing asceticism is something neither my sister nor I have expected, though in truth it's less asceticism than aversion to excess, to folds of skin that seem the physical expression of too easy a contentment. I still eat much more than my friends who are thinner, some of whom still wonder at my fondness for gustatory splendor. There is only a little less than there used to be of a woman who still wears too dark of lipstick, but to me this little makes a difference. Eating less of what looks like snow than I once did, I am allowing the inside of my body to become a warmer climate. What I don't tell my sister and anyone else who notices is this is the only virtue I can manage. I am making peace with the present, which allows for only so much sweetness.

I haven't yet decided if abandoning dessert after dinner is helping me to let go of other things, if I am also becoming lighter in other senses. I would like to think a lighter spirit, a less heavy presence, is this easy. I know I have experienced a certain satisfaction in not always rushing to fill my stomach, and sometimes I tell myself this is spiritual training. I tell myself I can better withstand emptiness now in other ways, if only because a lighter body better mimics the feeling of swimming even while I'm walking. It provides some of the same exhilaration the farmer in Scotland misses.

Only this is not the truth, not all of it. The truth is I also feel more attractive with less visible signs of contentment. Rather than having extra folds of skin hanging from my stomach, my body can now better communicate the fact I'm still hungry, still lusting. Even men grown big as cows themselves, who gorge themselves on sweetness, pass judgment on women who pay no attention to the size of their waists, their abdomens, their buttocks. I admit not wanting to be someone who puts on a bathing suit and whom men turn away from.

Once the pool party began in earnest—once my sister placed half a lion cake inside the cooler after my nephew opened all his presents—I left everyone else in the shallow end and swam several laps by myself in the deep end. I swam less in lines than in slaloms to avoid the clumps of teenagers bouncing on tiptoes, the young men and women feeling each other's bottoms. I left my sister and her husband to take my nephew down the slide, to savor his squealing and roars when he splashed them.

Next morning, I sat in my sister's yard while watching my nephew chase lizards as my younger niece stumbled with her arms outstretched behind him. Sitting beside me, my sister reached her hand out toward my hair, running her fingers through its ends. She was crossing her legs and drinking cold coffee. She set her cup down on the concrete and began braiding what she said was still so long and pretty. Then she let the ends drop abruptly, saying she had no rubber band to hold them. She sighed and threw her hands up, saying she had to feed the chickens. I felt my hair hang hot and unnecessary on my neck again.

My nephew and niece and I migrated to the front porch swing over the next few minutes, closer to my sister and the chickens. We looked for ladybugs while I asked them both to find gentlemenbugs to match them. My sister shouted from the henhouse for me to keep them there with me, to not come any closer—the bees were swarming again. In an ochre mass, the bees were flying toward a thicker group of grasses. Visibly shapeshifting, they were attempting to form another colony, to disperse and thin their supply of honey.

Tired of searching for the ladybugs' gentlemen, my nephew starting running toward the bees. I ran faster, though, and caught him before my sister panicked. Partly to distract him, I bent closer to his face and told him that my name means honeybee. I lowered my voice and said because of this I know when it's best to stay away from them, when they are apt to sting little boys who roar like a lion. He grabbed my hands then and asked me to swing him. He begged and told me his own name means farmer. When I asked how he knew this, he said his mom had told him. Together we were honey farmers, I concluded while spinning him until his legs swung level with his head, turning into the blades of a helicopter. Only the bees made all the honey, I admitted, which meant we did nothing. We had no profession other than avoiding being stung by them.

Moments later, my sister walked toward us carrying a dead chicken. The fence is electric, she said, so she didn't know how a coyote had gotten through it to leave the chicken's head hanging by a thread. This was her second death this week, she added. Too many for natural causes. She pointed with her free hand toward the tops of the sycamore trees and said the vultures were already circling overhead. I wondered aloud how they smelled the chicken from this distance. My sister shuddered, saying she would wrap the carcass in plastic until we could take it to the dump after we went to the market. Once you attract vultures, though, they never really leave, she said. Smell death once and they stay, keep looking.

When my dad was no older than my nephew and may himself have roared like a little lion, his tonsils were taken and never returned to him. He told me this when I was only five or six, when he was sitting on his organ bench inside our living room while no longer facing his organ. He told me this because I asked him, because I had discovered through a friend this was a way of eating nothing except ice cream for days on end. He said the cold had numbed the pain, and that was its purpose.

He told me this after he had finished his Saturday evening organ practice for Sunday's morning church service. He cast his gaze out over my dolls and crayons splayed across the carpet while folding his arms across the expanse of his stomach. He said there was too much clutter, something he said often, never accepting this as part of having children. This is what his tonsils also would have been to him once the pain receded, a part of me realized even then. Clutter in the mouth, pillows at the back of the throat no longer needed. Two soft masses flanking the pharynx and meant to fight infection. Only once they themselves become infected, they begin inflicting damage. Even before this, pits known as crypts extend throughout their tissue. A place of death then even while someone is living. A place of death, of something missing, even in newborn babies. While the vultures cried above our heads and my nephew begged me to spin him like he was becoming a helicopter again, I wondered if my own tonsils were removed whether I would eat the ice cream offered. I wondered if I would refuse what was meant to soothe me after the operation.

After his tonsils were taken, my dad didn't stay in a hospital again until he was diagnosed with the illness that killed him. Little as he ate throughout his treatment, throughout his months of bed rest, he never grew thin. If he lost five or ten pounds from chemotherapy, I never noticed. Though he seemed to like the male doctor who never cured him, he often complained about the female nurses, saying they were less attentive. Most took longer lunches, he said, than needed. They were all too casual, too contented with too little concern for their patients. They had too large of buttocks, waists, and abdomens. He imagined they did little after their shifts beyond watch TV series.

One Saturday afternoon when I visited, he said one nurse had forgotten to wipe ketchup off her chin. She had worn a beard looking like dried blood when she checked his pulse then helped him to the toilet. Like all the others, she took too long changing his catheter. Their added weight slowed them down, he added. He didn't want to imagine a single one of them wearing a bathing suit, he told a friend of his who arrived not long after I did. He didn't want to see any of these cows at the beach trying to swim. He'd as soon have his own Herefords brave the ocean. These women all talked too loudly and bordered on stupid. He said you had to be pretty dumb to let your body become that shapeless, when his friend laughed and nodded.

After his friend left, I stood to leave, sooner than I knew he wanted. As I put on my jacket, I reminded a dying man how he was little different from the nurses, how they shared a weight problem. I said through his recent remarks about their bodies he had isolated the reason for his own lack of intelligence. I told him that his comments were sexist then blamed him for my own slow metabolism. I freighted our lifeboat with excess baggage just as we were charting the rapids. Could I only forget this happened—could I only see him again and he observe how I've grown thinner, visibly less a person—I might grow lighter in other senses. Memory might be less a burden.

The man on the documentary from Scotland never said whether he lost any of his cows while making them swim from island to island. I assume, though, this happened. Presumably in all those decades one or two or more didn't make it to fresh grazing. There are always accidents, always some drownings even among calm waters. Yet the swim all in all must have been worth it—the swim not in summer but in spring then autumn, when the water could hardly have been a balm from the heat that never truly comes to northern Scotland. If swimming to fresh pastures had not meant starvation, then it meant becoming leaner when cows are intended to be bred fat for slaughter.

My dad had been forced to sell his own herd by the time he had grown sick enough to complain about the nurses. Large as he still looked compared to the average, solid as he still appeared of a Midwestern farmer, he was too weak to shepherd them from one pasture to the next as he had done for decades before this. His arms had gone too soft to feed them. The pastures we could glimpse from our kitchen stayed vacant as he lay in a hospital where all the nurses had too big of bottoms. The pastures became crypts for all intents and purposes, with no more animals to feed from their grasses. I did nothing to compensate for his beloved cows' absence, offered him no sweetness. After I heard my dad telling his friend about the fat nurses, I left the hospital pinching my abdomen.

Before dinner on my last evening at my sister's, she said she wanted to give me some honey to take back to Chicago. She said I could drizzle it on my cereal in the mornings, sweeten whatever I wanted. Mentioning she needed to check on the bees again, she asked her husband if she should wear the beekeeper's suit, maybe just the helmet with netting. She asked him, I believe, because of the intensity of the heat, because she didn't want to wear anything more than necessary, because she wanted someone else's permission for using the smoker alone. Her husband nodded, agreeing she didn't need to wear more clothing, as he jiggled their daughter on his knee. He said he had to change her diaper while I chased my nephew through the sprinklers for relief from the humidity.

Moments later, my sister ran back screaming she had been stung, not once or twice but twenty or more times, all across the bare topography of her arms and legs. The welts immediately started appearing, swelling as she cried aloud in anguish. She left us to go shower after asking her husband to help extract the stingers implanted in her skin like seedlings in a garden. As she ran to the bathroom, she handed me a shard of honeycomb. Eat it, she almost shouted at me. I started to suck the honey from the wax directly as if doing so might soothe her pain. These stings from her wild bees, I felt she meant, should amount to something.

I savored honey suffused with a more delicate sweetness than I remembered it being as the shower offered my sister a brief, mild respite. I savored the honey's taste and texture then began eating the comb with it. I was uncertain whether leaving any of the beeswax that had stored the liquid would upset her, so I forced it all down my stomach. Seeing my face as I bit into the last of it ten minutes later, she said there was no problem. I could eat it—fresh beeswax was delicious. Then she threw herself onto the couch and said the worst part of bee stings was resisting the urge to scratch them. I nodded even though I have not been stung by a bee in decades. I can hardly remember the sensation.

That night, she couldn't sleep from the itching. She told me this the next morning, the day I was leaving, with all her limbs swollen to nearly twice their normal size. My niece, she added, still cries for hours late into the early morning since my sister has stopped breastfeeding. My sister never gets to sleep through the night anyway then. Her life, I acknowledged, was hard in so many ways I could not fathom. Mine is so empty in comparison. Not to needlessly fill it has become its own challenge.

Putting her hair into braids as she made us eggs laid by her chickens for breakfast, my sister mentioned she has read that some people use bee stings as therapy. Most of those who do this suffer from arthritis or multiple sclerosis. Some, though, simply absorb the stings as preventative medication. They claim the pain of this prevents that in future should they be stung again. Pouring myself a cup of coffee, I said I'd still avoid it, and she agreed this was wisest. She sighed and said she hadn't meant to do this.

After he finished his breakfast, my nephew sat on the organ bench and began to play it. He flipped the same switch my dad did for decades, every Saturday evening before Sunday's service. My nephew cannot play music, cannot even reach the pedals, but he pounded away at the keys with abandonment. Singing to himself as he sounded a reel without a melody, he seemed contented in a way I can barely remember being. Looking up from wiping my niece's chin, my sister told him the grandfather he had never met and Aunt Melissa were both musicians.

I haven't played in too many years to remember, I responded. I hardly even listen much to music. By high school, I was already done playing duets on the organ with my dad at Christmas. As my hips began to widen, the organ bench grew too crowded. As my nephew sounded his disharmony, I hugged him then grabbed my luggage.

Temperatures had reached the mid-nineties by the time I left the airport in Indianapolis. Still sitting on the plane, I shivered in the air conditioning. I wished I had a sweater with me and realized that were my nephew only born in winter, my sister would have gotten no bee stings. Were my nephew only conceived in warmer weather and born nine months later, I would never have told him that my name means honeybee. I would never have learned that his means farmer, that together we are honey farmers who get no bee stings and grow no stronger.

It is August now, when my dad would urge me to swim in Lake Michigan rather than sit inside with the curtains closed to the scaffolding climbing my apartment building. He would tell me to go to the beach instead. I can almost hear him saying it, pointing me toward the pleasure I'm resisting. It will be cold enough soon, he would tell me while forgetting I prefer the cold to the heat, forgetting there is such a thing as winter honey, forgetting that life offers its share of sweetness even when all the world looks frozen. Still I can hear him urging me outside as I sit in my armchair with my beach towel covering my legs in the air conditioning. Approaching summer's end, they still look as white as if snow had just melted over top of them.

Even if my dad is trying from beyond the grave to tell me to take advantage of the summer that is waning, this doesn't mean he knows everything. This doesn't mean he hears the lifeguards blow their whistles when I eventually do as he asks and have walked with my towel to the lake. This doesn't mean he hears them shouting I've gone too far into the deep waters when I've only waded in up to my waist. He doesn't see that swimming in water shallow enough to walk in—swimming around children in slaloms—is no real swimming to begin with. I leave the lake without the pleasure of exertion.

My only option to do as he wishes is to enter the waves after sunset when the lifeguards have all gone home. Two nights ago, I let the waves carry me out farther than I have ever been before driving me harder toward the sand again. I let the waves pretend to heal me then leave me breathless. While being swallowed by the current, afraid my life might be ending with the last of the daylight, I looked out toward the wall of high-rises, a wall too large to disappear on the horizon.

HORRIPILATION

PLAYING DRESS-UP

Prague

Something about the golem reminded me of my dad. Something in its silence, though my dad had always been talkative. Both had the same round stomachs, copper complexions. The golem standing beside me was only a metal sculpture, twin holes for eyes punched inside its head, elbows rusted. If my dad were to come to life again, he would look something like this. Only he would have tree branches for bone, mud for muscles dissolving as easily as they harden. He would look closer to those golems of legend, made of earth alone, than the man I remember—dark eyebrows running together, legs thin compared to the rest of him—and whom I still resemble more than any other person.

Unrecognizable as I'd now find him, he would find me changed as well, an older woman than the one he left—my hair

179

thinner, my face folded in places—though still with his same profile, same facial expressions, even if my dad is now all but faceless. Finding a quiet place to sit amid crowded places, I sometimes imagine he fills the silence with his essence while knowing his essence to be no more than the clay that makes a golem. A man who is hardly recognized outside the Czech Republic.

No grass blanketed the patio dividing our hotel from a hostel looking little different. Its concrete was carpeted with plastic turf instead, greener than real grass, without insects or pollen. In the corner farthest from the entrance, the golem stood naked, caring nothing for those taking pictures of themselves squeezed inside his armpit. Unlike the plastic grass blades at his feet and those who kept flattening them, he didn't bother disguising who he was at bottom by wearing any clothing, by speaking of where he had traveled before this. Two young women sitting at the picnic table across from me were smoking, speaking loudly in English. They tapped ashes onto grass where nothing was growing from below it.

Pretending to read a magazine someone else had left, I stared down at yellow leaves fallen from a tree potted in a vase too shallow for its root system. I disliked the women's jagged voices, the smell of tobacco staining the air around them. I watched the early autumn leaves spin in gentle eddies, leaves prevented by the turf from dissolving into the earth below the concrete, from returning home again. Yet earth remains endlessly receptive, allowing concrete to suffocate it of oxygen, allowing anything with feet to trod it into hardness. The earth often does nothing except swallow another body once it tires of breathing. It remains indifferent to whether the body once spoke softly, held doors open for the elderly. The two young women both ignored the nearly crippled gentleman I helped to walk up the steps and rest beside them. The earth did the same, offered no opinion while seeing little to distinguish women sitting on similar picnic benches. Instead, it only waits to hush, absorb them.

On our second day in Prague, my husband walked back to our hotel to rest after we trundled up the hill to the castle together and then back down it. He tends to grow tired during the day when we're traveling, whereas I normally want to keep exploring and don't mind doing so without him. Almost as soon as we separated, several street merchants tried selling me small crystal vials of fluid. Swallow and they said I'd become a different person. They had no way of knowing how much I wanted this, had even less real ability to make this happen. Still they kept walking beside me, hanging their wares from their wrists. Still they made a living trading on the memory of long dead alchemists, though they must have known few would believe their promise.

One man wearing an eye patch followed me past Charles Bridge, making me offers for better prices. He said I could hang the emptied vial from a necklace. I shook my head, moving past him through the throngs of other tourists. I felt for change in my wallet then bought raspberries from a man also selling small wooden carvings of the astronomical clock whose clockmaker was blinded so his handiwork could not be replicated. Handing me my change, the merchant relayed the legend, hoping I'd also buy a small clock that told no time from him. The clockmaker himself has so long vanished that his suffering now seems harmless.

My raspberries eaten, my fingers stained red with their remnants, I turned in a direction from Old Town Square I had not yet taken. I walked until I found a small Imaginarium, a funhouse made for children. Inside its basement, I wended my way through a labyrinth whose walls were made of mirrors, a room designed to lose yourself among hundreds of your own reflections. A woman handed me plastic gloves at its entrance so I could feel my way through to the end without smudging the mirrors' faces, so I could finger my own image without leaving any evidence I was here for the next person.

From certain angles, I hardly recognized a woman whose face hung slack, her lips a little slanted. Her glasses hid half her face while the black dress falling past her knees made her seem modest. Only I knew how much she liked being noticed, how she still thought there was something to be gained from this, how often she confused who she really was with her reflection. In Prague, the only men who had spoken to her besides her husband tried to convince her to become another person, and she couldn't help reading something into this. Had she only seen herself as they did, her lips tilted without her knowledge, she might have bought a vial of fluid. As it was, the city's beauty left her distracted.

I walked through the mirror maze more quickly than the woman at the desk told me she had expected, faster than most people managed. Passing a small museum of alchemy ten minutes after this, I browsed its gift shop but decided against paying the fee for admission. I decided against touring the laboratories, spending yet more time in darkened places on a day this sunny. From the brochure I was handed, they looked to be candlelit caverns, places of hiding, while the azure sky above them remained cloudless. The alchemists also never converted base metal into something more alluring, never created the youth elixir they promised. All they succeeded in was living out most of their lives half buried, working closer to the earth than the heavens, closer to where the only real transformation ever happens. Like my husband still sleeping, they missed the daylight, the fountains. They missed the raspberries.

Turning down another side street, I walked past a shop selling women's used clothing. I walked past then back inside, across a threshold overhung with nacreous windchimes, singing and dangling. I found the shop by accident but was aware some part of me had also been searching for a way of becoming, if not a different woman, then one who looked less modest. The woman behind the counter had overdrawn her eyelids with so much darkness they looked mapped with bruises, with violence. To the many dresses hanging in a protective caul around her, she seemed unresponsive. She yawned as she greeted me in English, likely judging my clothing as American. She wore only a T-shirt and jeans, needed nothing beyond this to look pretty, her blackened eyes unable to diminish what she had been given without her asking. I walked past her while inhaling the light mold suggesting other women had once been beautiful inside dresses now hung without regard to similar color or sizing.

Behind a velvet curtain, I tried on a cream-colored dress whose fabric my husband later said felt like terrycloth when he fingered its folds, its selvage. It falls loosely from my shoulders and is structured at the waist by a belt looking like a pastel, slim mosaic. When I turned before a mirror no one else saw me in, the dress told me the same lie I hear over and over again even when I'm naked, the lie that always makes a new dress feel like new skin, the lie I always find reassuring, even when someone else has worn the dress before me. Here at last is something to make me worth seeing, ending the isolation of living in a separate body. Here is a dress that reveals the inner beauty never quite rising to the surface. No longer a farmer's daughter because my farmer father is dead and buried, no longer forced to dirty my hands and wear old clothing, I can wear another dress in another city where I can become another woman, however briefly. I can keep buying nicer ones until the earth swallows me whole, makes me into a golem.

An hour later as I sat on the patio pretending to read a magazine while waiting for my husband to wake from his sleep, the golem kept silent even when I turned for him to notice the dress I hoped made me look more European. The golem alone, though, knows I am not the dress but the skin beneath it. No, the organs beneath the skin. No, the skeleton. No, the earth that pays no attention to whether I hold doors open, my voice soft spoken. I buy so many more dresses than needed because a lie must work hard to appear less of an illusion. Whereas the truth needs no defense, no explanation, no clothing. The golem stays silent, stands naked for a reason.

Only while I'm still lying, while I'm still busy disguising my essence, my body continues responding to certain textures, certain fabrics with horripilation, a bristling of hair on skin better known as gooseflesh. The phenomenon once made our ancestors appear larger when faced with danger but now occurs with something closer to love more often, closer to its promise than its presence. My skin grows its small mountains, makes hair stand on end. My skin falls in love with the lie the dress is telling, falls but never lands on any surface. Instead, it only shivers with the dress's novelty, a feature that grows more attractive the longer you remain the same person. I wore the terrycloth dress out to eat in Prague for the next two evenings. I noticed men noticing me and knew the dress was the reason. A lie told to escape the truth of the golem.

Montreal

THERE IS a pale pink dress printed with black butterflies that has hung inside my closet for almost two decades. It has been out of style since the late 1980s. Even then, it would have fallen too high on my waist, had I yet grown into a woman's body. The one time I tried it on at my mom's gentle insistence, it padded my shoulders that needed no padding, widened my hips in no need of widening, while my mom wore it only once as I remember. She slipped inside its silken skin when we went out to eat on what must have been Easter Sunday, because I can still see daffodils out the corners of my vision, the dress's pink sky glimmering even amid the daylight's brightness. She had not needed to wear a coat when we were leaving the restaurant, crossing the street to our car. We grew so much of our own food that we only ever ate out on holidays.

The sky the butterflies flew against deepened my mom's already tan complexion. It was the only dress she ever wore to my way of seeing that accentuated rather than hid her beauty, the only one that might have been remotely conceived of as provocative, though to me it still seems modest. Whenever I expressed my desire for her to wear it again, she said she felt it was too glamorous for her life at the moment, for the small town we prayed and went to school in, which tells me that one Easter when she wore it we must have driven to Indianapolis. She spent too much time in the fields and garden, batting flies from her eyelids while being deafened by diesel tractor engines, to ever justify its expense. A shame, she admitted. At day's end, her fingernails were usually blackened with dirt beneath the edges. Over the years, she also gained some weight, said she could no longer zip it. When she gave it to me shortly after I finished college, she said my dad had taken her shopping not long after they were married. An extravagance he never repeated to my knowledge.

Some part of her had likely hoped my life would offer me more opportunities to wear it, a hope that must have blinded her to changes in fashion. Still the dress is the only one hung inside my closet I know to be honest, incapable of telling the same lie told by all the others, incapable for being unflattering. Its butterflies are no butterflies at all, it has tried telling me, though I have only begun to listen. Its butterflies are not black but missing. Butterfly-shaped holes instead of winged insects, they are only what's left when the real ones succeeded in puncturing the pink sky behind them. The real butterflies have flown to some world beyond this.

Although I wear nicer clothing now than either of my parents, I cannot say it has solved anything. Even in the world's most beautiful cities, I have never escaped who I am at bottom, a farmer's daughter who now never dirties her fingertips, who spends her life moving only through crowded places. I cannot say any of the dresses I have bought online late into the evening have ever made me feel at home inside this body. Since both my parents died what I still view as far too early, home has been no more to me than this skin. No longer a particular place or set of faces, home has meant only this body, though part of me still longs to leave it, to leap outside this prison into someone else's, to be seen more clearly, to be taller, more attractive. I used to feel guilty for wasting money on clothes my husband doesn't need to tell me are unnecessary, but the earth remains indifferent, knows what's coming.

A couple hours after my plane landed in Montreal, I texted my husband a picture of a geodesic dome designed by Buckminster Fuller resting on St. Helen's Island. Before I left, he made me promise to go see it, though he himself was flying in only a few days later. Almost immediately he texted back, You made it! though I hadn't. I had stayed on the mainland, only zoomed my camera in after deciding not to take the ferry across the St. Lawrence River, not to spend the time there I could spend better in ways I wanted, doing next to nothing. My husband considers Fuller a visionary, says he solved a myriad of problems related to energy and housing, but this man my husband almost worships had not done anything for me as I saw it. I owed him nothing. Still I stayed standing there a moment as light rain started to fall. No one walked or stood beside me. Aside from the seagulls' cries, all was silence.

I had no reason for being in Montreal to begin with, no more than I have for buying dresses whose butterflies may always fly through their fabric. I have accepted, though, serving no real purpose, only drifting. There was nothing in the city I particularly wanted to see. I only wanted to walk unfamiliar streets where people were speaking a foreign language so I couldn't understand what they were saying, so I could better focus on their faces. Flying somewhere for relatively cheap, I still wanted to enjoy the mystery of being a woman again in a strange city, of moving through crowds while having nowhere I needed to be, walking so slowly compared to the natives that I become as motionless as the sky behind them. My first evening, I ate in a Polish restaurant near the room I rented for five evenings, though near our apartment there are similar Polish places with better food, all less expensive. Outside, construction crews were working late. Ceaseless drilling.

Buckminster Fuller nearly killed himself while living in Chicago, where I have lived now for nearly half of my existence, after his young daughter died from polio complications. He had lost his job and begun drinking heavily when his wife gave birth again. Knowing his suicide would allow her to collect his life insurance, he was walking along Lake Michigan, planning to swim until he drowned from exhaustion. Only as soon as he resolved himself to diving in, a voice without a body attached to it spoke to him, saying he belonged to the universe more than to his family. He belonged to something so much larger than he could imagine, the voice insisted. His isolation, his seemingly separate body, the voice pronounced an illusion. The voice gave the impression of knowing everything, of descending from the heavens. Because I've never had a similar experience, I cannot give Fuller's any credence. It is likely for this reason I tend to trust only the silence below me.

Spiderwebs can float in a hurricane, Fuller later grew fond of observing. He wanted the geodesic domes he patented to become nearly as durable and lightweight, to the point airplanes could carry their kits across countries. His domes would offer shelter for refugees fleeing war-torn countries, for which, like my husband, I can applaud him as a visionary. Only this never materialized. He predicted at least a million would be built across the country by the mid-1980s. The number instead topped out at roughly 300,000 globally by the early 1990s. Since then, their popularity has only further diminished. Montreal's only one has been made into a museum. Most of our houses have remained rooted in the earth, all too solid.

The voice that spoke to him may have enjoyed a higher perspective, seeing bodies as only illusion. But until our bones, our tendons dissolve into phantasms, becoming weightless, the body remains our primary home, the walls in which the body sleeps, cooks, bathes far secondary. Fuller in his love for his own invention also failed to account for the fact the body is mobile already, all too easily capable of boarding airplanes to other cities. He seemed to have altogether forgotten the allure of leaving your permanent mailing address for other places. Fuller must have either never known or related to the pleasure of flying while still seated among strangers who hardly care about your life somewhere else altogether, about how you decorate your bedroom or kitchen.

Walking through the cobblestone streets of Old Montreal a couple hours before my husband flew in, I stepped inside a clothing shop where I tried on two dresses. Each one was made from the same print, but they fell to two different lengths, suggesting they were made for two different kinds of women. Both their skies were equally stark a white, a solid cloud tapestry. Butterflies printed over top the clouds were bright and golden, still alive and flying. Both dresses fit me, but the saleswoman preferred the shorter, said that I should buy it. This wasn't, she said, a sale that lasted.

Her accent sounded vaguely Slavic. Though I had no way of knowing how long ago she had left her native country for Canada, the fact she had done so gave her ample justification for considering herself homeless even while she stood before me, well-dressed and taking my money. If she were unable to return to her home, if she were a refugee, this was only more reason from her perspective for me to buy another dress almost too small for me. A woman only growing older every second may at any time find herself homeless, her body unrecognizable and insufficient compared to what it had been. Clothes too at bottom are only protection from the elements.

She pulled the dress down lower over my hips so the neckline also dipped. She nodded her head, said I had a nice body. The dress was more flattering, she added, for more skin showing. I turned in front of a mirror that I felt reflected a woman more attractive than the one who walked in ten minutes before this. I asked if I could wear it out, feeling at home again in a dress of my liking whose butterflies still flew across their fabric. When my husband saw me wearing it later that evening, he said it showed too much skin, looked made for a younger woman. I have not worn it again. More money wasted.

It was the weekend before Halloween and twenty degrees warmer than average. Neither my husband nor I needed to wear a jacket when we walked along the Old Port in the evening, where garage bands were playing, where we ate Indian food with our fingers and listened then danced once we were finished eating. Although no children were trick-or-treating, more than half the teenagers were in costume, wearing masks of monsters or the too short dresses of French maids and Bavarian women. Action heroes in spandex. A man with a plastic axe through his head asked me in passing who I was supposed to be. I had nothing to tell him. I realized the golden butterflies were little different from those black ones that had gone missing against a pinker sky before this. I was dressed only as someone still wanting to be noticed, only half succeeding.

Sunday morning, we took the bus to Mount Royal to eat pierogies in the grass and listen to the drum circle that gathered here every week as long as the weather was decent. A snaking waterslide, a makeshift tongue of plastic, ran down a hill large as a small mountain. I wanted to slide down it but hadn't worn a bathing suit, which would have been better for sliding. In the surging heat of late October, many had, however. Several of the same men and women who had likely also been at the Old Port last evening had taken off their costumes, wore little more now than their skin, their homes as portable as Buckminster Fuller could wish it. They played the drums to the rhythm of their heartbeats, and again I wore the dress with the butterflies that were alive and flying. My husband laughed at how overdressed I was compared to those beating both real drums and only buckets, those falling down a waterslide and those who were only dancing barefoot, the women's legs loose at the knees, unshaven. As the day wore on, the drums grew deafening. My legs overspread with gooseflesh. When the time came to leave, I was chilly. I had exhausted the city's promise.

Chicago

I WAKE now each morning with new lines drawn across my arms, my thighs, my neck. Long, red etchings, scrimshaw on skin. Artwork no one else notices. The ends of the lines tend to bend. My husband bites his nails down to nubbins, so he is not to blame for this. My nails are also shorter than most women's, though each morning there is the same fresh evidence I have scraped myself in my sleep again. As they start healing, the lines resemble stitches that stitch together what was already unbroken. I try to show my husband, but he always starts talking about something more important, ignoring what he thinks of as my need for attention. Because I live alone inside this body, I alone am attuned to its moods, its muscle contractions. In return, my skin alone is sympathetic as I walk amid crowded places, bristling with promise that something may still be different.

Last weekend, we went to a wedding, the first we have been to in several years, as most people our age are already married or have long decided against it. The friend who invited me is one I've largely lost touch with, though our lives are not much different than before we stopped calling, texting, having lunch on a regular basis. We both live in the same apartments, only half an hour away by public transportation. Taking too much comfort in silence, spending too much time in foreign places, has its consequences as well as consolations.

The ceremony took place in the same room as the reception, at a bar better known for its live music. I'd worn a dress of deep purple with black trim, revealing my arms, my skin below my collarbone for the first time in several months, as we were now approaching winter's end. An uncertain time with light snowfall followed by shifting winds.

When I smiled and congratulated her husband, he didn't recognize my face. I felt certain of this until he danced with his mother as I joined the circle enfolding them. I watched him hold her wrists, their movements tender and stiff, then realized he may have ignored me on purpose. He may have done the same as I had done to him about a month before this. Late January in LaGuardia on a Sunday afternoon, I had seen him rest his hands on my friend's shoulders. He had started pulling some her of hair from her bun, almost spilling it into a chestnut fountain, as she laughed, swatting away his fingers. I saw them sitting, taking pictures of each other while resting an arm or leg on their luggage. I watched their spines slacken against their seats, their casual contentment inside bodies they have both let grow larger through the years without caring, both wearing their clothes more loosely to only half hide this. I walked and sat facing the window at another gate than the one immediately beside where they were sitting. I held a book to my face as I turned away from them. I had wanted to walk closer, buy a bottle of water. Instead I slumped, stayed thirsty.

Sunday evening, and we were both flying back to Chicago from New York City. Until they stood in line to board a flight that took off half an hour before mine, their backs both toward me, I held the muscles in my jaw as if fighting to preserve my silence, while a little girl seated across from me kept crying, wanting more of a candy bar than she was given. My friend and her then boyfriend would likely suffer the same turbulence throughout the same storm system. They were a couple, while I had left my husband for the weekend to visit a friend. I had caught a cold sleeping on the floor of her apartment in Manhattan but had worn one of my better fitting sweater dresses among a vaster sea of faces. Today, I was wearing jeans with a cotton dress over top of it, one with bright orange palm leaves wrapped across an olive firmament. Something better suited for autumn, though the weather was warm for the season.

If I had walked and bought the water I wanted, had simply said hello to people I may now never see again, I could have rescued our friendship, given the groom reason to remember me at the reception. I could have conjured the magic of coincidence. As it was, I coughed as quietly as I could into my book, was having trouble breathing through my sinuses. I looked again at the face of the little girl still begging for more candy and asked myself who I was dressing for if not for someone I knew, someone sitting only the next gate over, closer to the runway. Sunday night back in my apartment, I said nearly nothing to my husband and went to bed early.

At the wedding, I saw several other friends who were more acquaintances and felt like a stranger among them. When I told the bride she looked beautiful and radiant, she hugged me briefly, moved on to people she could better enjoy her time with. I tried telling her I had bought her a bubble machine as well as the duvet she listed on her registry. I said she could unwrap the bubble machine now and use it. I pointed to where it sat on the table beside a plate stacked with cupcakes, but she politely ignored the comment. On the stage where bands played most weekends, a photographer stood beside a life-size cardboard cutout of a popu-lar musician in sunglasses. One group of friends then couple after another drunkenly posed for black-and-white pictures, which flashed throughout the evening on a TV screen. I stayed dancing on the floor just beneath the stage, watched them knowing myself to be one of the better dressed of the women. I had secretly wanted my husband to snap a picture of me with his phone, but he didn't.

Watching the parade of bodies above me while I danced in the shadow space below them, I became the earth while the woman I normally was went missing. I swallowed all the other bodies and grew receptive. They walked above my head, suffocating me of oxygen, and I felt something deeply painful inside me contracting. A single, small muscle below the skin, one so small no one can see it until thousands of others do the same, until thousands of more hairs stand on end. I felt homeless, unattached to my body. I shouted the lyrics of the song that was playing. Because everyone else was doing the same, no one heard me.

My husband pulled my arm with the most scratches, insisting we take our turn and have our picture taken. I shook my head, but he still pulled me on stage with him. In the image that later flashed on the TV screen, my face looked empty. I didn't recognize this woman. Black-and-white photography works best with people whose features speak more loudly while mine are soft-spoken. Without the purple of my dress to deepen my complexion, I bled into the background curtain, almost disappearing.

In what still feels like a small hallucination, a man with watery eyes and lips that seemed to speak without moving started dancing near me as my husband left for the bar to buy another beer. A man I found almost unbearably handsome looked into my face with an intensity that seemed related to what causes me to scrape my skin in yet more places each evening. He came closer and asked me if we had met before, three years ago maybe. He named the concert where it had been, before I had lost touch with the bride, before he moved to Brooklyn. He said the bride and groom had both visited him about a month before this. If I hadn't ignored them at LaGuardia, I realized I could have told him of the coincidence.

He asked me if I had been here the whole time, and I nodded. He said he didn't believe it, and I could tell he wanted to ask more questions. Instead, his eyes took me in. For the first time and what may likely be the end, I felt fully seen in a place this crowded. He bent down to my ear and said he liked my dress, said he still remembered the one I had worn the other time we met, red and flared at the hips. He leaned in closer again and asked if I was here with anyone, and I nodded toward my husband, who by this time had started dancing with another woman.

As he looked at me, he asked me my name again. I felt my face, my whole body soften. Watching the waters in his eyes deepen, I realized the reason I have bought so many dresses is only to imagine being undressed by men looking exactly like this. The lie they tell is also one of freedom, those rare occasions when an inner beauty almost rises to the surface. During these few and fleeting moments, I knew even as they were receding, the lie meant nothing while meaning everything. In Brooklyn, I also realize this kind of thing is all too common. He was only doing what had become a habit.

I walked to the bar for a glass of water, to ease my thirst and also have a reason to stop dancing between my husband and the man toward whom I felt myself moving closer, both of them illusions. My husband stayed, and the other followed me. Away

193

from the music, he spoke softly. He asked me if I still lived here, when I nodded. He said he had never heard anything more about me after that one evening. I couldn't remember what we had said three years before this, only that a quiet place had been carved inside me then. A place as dark as a closet filled with dresses he will never see me wearing. A place I have always needed. Before I left the reception with my husband, I turned around at the entrance. I told him I forgot something.

Taking one last look at someone I'll never see again, I did so as slowly as some hibernating sea creature rising from the bottom of the ocean, immense and naked. As I pretended to look for a scarf kept inside my pocket, I hoped he was watching, though by then he may have turned toward other women. Still the day after the wedding, I felt like I was floating. Another day afterward, I had sunk into a deeper silence. My body grew heavy, my home more solid. As I had said goodbye to him, I remembered he had looked into my face then down toward my arm's scratches. He ran his hand across the skin, smooth except for the lines of dried blood, the wounds I make while sleeping. As he traced each small muscle covered by a hair follicle, it raised, contracted.

When the voice spoke to Buckminster Fuller on the shores of Lake Michigan, Fuller later reported he had been suspended several feet above the ground. He claimed he was enclosed in a sphere of sparkling light, and I have no reason to not believe him. This experience more than likely served as a model for his geodesic domes, which we have hardly made use of as intended. I also suspect his body too felt lighter after this. I suspect he felt more at home there, making houses' mobility seem yet more important, making him blind to the fact people still might prefer theirs grounded in earth remaining incapable of judgment. Only receptive, waiting.

DARWIN'S TUBERCLE

SOFTER HEARING

The last time I saw her was in a grocery store when I was on winter break during my sophomore year of college. We had grown up together but were never friends, probably because we had both too much and too little in common. Both our fathers were farmers. Both of us were older sisters with younger sisters of the same age, both of whom were milder mannered than we had ever been. In the grocery store only a mile away from where we had gone to grammar school together, I was buying milk and bread for my parents. Amy was doing something similar, I imagined. I didn't know where she went to college, what she studied or for what reason. She would be practical, though, about it. We had breathed enough of the same oxygen for enough years on end for me to know this was her gift and her essence. A narrowing of possibilities that made life more certain.

As we walked toward opposite sides of the same mounds of apples and colorless melons, Amy narrowed her eyebrows as our eyes met. I smiled, and she turned her cart away, avoiding conversation. She made a point of ignoring me even though we never had a conflict. We had known each other from the age of five through the same passive and daily process of absorption with which we had once become all too intimately acquainted with the cinderblock walls of our classrooms, with their every chip of paint and crevice. Over the years and owing to the smallness of our grammar school when we had known each other most closely, we had studied each other along with everyone else around us while largely lacking awareness of our own observation. Through the course of daily spelling lessons and gym classes, of standing in line to wait for lunch and recess, we had digested far too much information about each other's personalities, the import of every movement, for me to fail to appreciate she was trying to punish me, although for unknown reasons.

Back in southern Indiana again, Amy knew as little of my life in Chicago as I did of hers, wherever she now lived, though she may have made her guesses. Over the years, she may have easily formed opinions about me of which I remained unconscious, about which even if I knew I might not have cared regardless. I watched her push her cart toward the checkout counter, realizing that since grammar school had ended we had rarely looked into each other's faces. Although I knew her eyes were light in color, I could not have said whether they were blue or green exactly. Although I recognized her easily from a distance, her features blurred together the moment she turned her head away from me, her nose and chin becoming shapeless. Amy disappeared, marching through the sliding glass doors with her groceries, and it didn't make a difference.

As far as I was concerned, she had already fulfilled her purpose. Time and again, she had reminded me to soften. She had done this without knowing, simply by her presence, from the time we were in kindergarten. She had done this by embodying hardness, by showing me what could happen if I did the same, if I held in too many negative emotions and became the kind of person who ignored people beside the produce section for the sake of making them feel smaller, unimportant. Even if I didn't know why she had chosen to do this, I also understood it was part of her from almost the beginning. She had always been more like a cinderblock wall than anyone else in any of my classes. Even as a child, there had been an intransigence, a stiffness I also recognize as part of who I am, who I can be.

Decades have now passed since I last saw her on winter break from college. I have thought of her recently only because I am reminding myself to soften again. For me, staying flexible in several senses has become a healing practice, the equivalent of feeling myself dissolve among crowds of people like powdered medicine in a glass of liquid. Especially as I have grown older, I have recognized the tendency of the body and mind to stiffen, to trade mystery for certainty, to rely on assumptions acquired over the course of decades rather than experience life in the present, the only place ever allowing for freedom of movement. Mystery whenever I make room for it feels far more necessary, its own form of medicine, than the comfort of feeling I know what will happen in the next moment.

As a way of retraining myself to live more softly, freer of assumptions, I have recently begun walking through seas of anonymous faces while trying not to distinguish between beauty and ugliness, trying to free myself of the judgments based on appearances that arise almost unconsciously, even among people I will never speak with. I have begun trying to become more of a witness while walking in silence, a witness without opinions. Becoming more space, less of a person, now feels close to my life's purpose. Shedding some of my old tendencies toward judgment, letting go to some extent of old preferences and aversions, has made my own personality less a burden, has made this mind and body I am forced to inhabit less confining and more open. I have begun at least to try this, knowing I am still very hard in places. It was never saying much using Amy as a basis of comparison.

Growing up, I often avoided committing small sins or sooner stopped them because I didn't want to wake one day and find myself remade in Amy's same image. Because of her alone, I sometimes stopped shouting at my sister, resisted eating so much that my stomach protruded with excess consumption. For the most part, I preserved my manners and compassion, never developed as round a stomach or bottom as I could have. Because of someone who seemed as hard to me as Amy from our earliest ages, who seemed to have cut herself off from mystery far too early, I avoided thrusting my lower lip out when I didn't like something. I know I never wiggled my ears in the lunch line for attention while the rest of my head stayed stationary. I never did this last thing partially because I couldn't perform this same trick even if I wanted. It was Amy's particular talent, and I quickly grew tired of seeing while trying to ignore it.

In the grocery store, as her figure receded, her movements betrayed the same stiffness that had always made me feel she had two bodies, one I could see and one I almost couldn't. The first was made of pale, wobbly jelly. The second was closer to an exoskeleton whose visibility was still evolving. To me, this girl I had grown up with had always been an organism housed within the frame of a building. Near the produce section, her muscles looked to have melded themselves into an even thicker armor. She looked to have become more, not less, of someone for whom I always felt an instinctive revulsion. A space for beauty then. If not for beauty alone, then space for becoming something different than she had always been to me. Only now do I see I never gave her this. Perhaps if I had, she would have said hello, have never ignored me. Hard as she seemed, there must have been a part of her also wanting softness.

WHEN WINTER break of my sophomore year of college ended, my roommate walked into the kitchen and told me she was moving back to Minneapolis. I was washing dishes as she took the milk from the fridge then drank from the carton. She set the milk down on the counter and said she was going to save some money, live for a while with her parents. She didn't like Chicago, she decided, and was planning to leave before the month's end. She was going to take the rest of the semester off and then enroll in a community college. It took me a little time to digest this, to realize that by saving herself money, Sam was creating a financial predicament for me. During our last weeks as roommates, she seemed unconscious that paying the whole rent was something I might struggle with.

Her bright green eyes and glowing skin also seemed evidence of an inner radiance, one I felt myself lacking. Partly because of the disparity in our attractiveness, because hers seemed to lend her an innate authority, I never reminded her what her moving cost me. Her face still looms vivid in my memory whenever I take time to picture it. I never needed to create a space for beauty for her because her beauty was so obvious. As someone who practiced yoga on a daily basis, as someone whose silhouette was slim and shapely, Sam often mentioned I had an energy blockage, something hard that kept life's essence from flowing smoothly through me. While all her chakras worked in alignment, I often had neck pain, trouble sleeping. While her skin looked poreless, I still occasionally broke out with acne.

I didn't know what might have interrupted my flow of energy, what Sam could see that I couldn't. I had no idea then that softening was something I could practice, becoming a little more spacious, feeling a little less solid, simply through passing through crowds of people without appraisal or opinions. But I knew my hair was the color of wheat ripening in autumn, whereas Sam dyed hers a darker red more easily noticed from a distance. I knew when I walked beside her that she received all of the attention. All the space for beauty between us she had filled and taken. I told her I would miss her once she left, though not long after she did I realized how airless our apartment had been with her inside it. I opened all the windows, let the breeze flow in.

It wasn't until a couple weeks after she moved home again that Sam called and told me about Adam. A boy I had fallen a little in love with, who had lived on the floor above us in the dorm where Sam and I met, Adam was someone she had been sleeping with for months now, for ages. I never suspected, partly because Adam had a girlfriend a couple years older than him, a graduate student who taught one of his classes. Sam said she visited his dorm room at night while we were still freshmen. In recent months, she had gone to his apartment in the afternoons more often. After tracing the line of her spinal column and telling her she had a beautiful body, she said he sometimes cried thinking of how he was betraying his girlfriend. The fact he never left her was part of the reason she decided to move back to Minneapolis.

Instead of looking for another roommate to pay her half of the rent, I took on extra waitressing shifts at the diner where I had been working only weekends before Sam left. Once my lease ended, I found a smaller, less expensive apartment. Once I had a taste of freedom, I didn't want to relinquish it. I didn't want someone else to fill the space I now knew I needed for something inside me—something akin to inner quiet, to air that stayed with me and I wasn't forced to always breathe out and then in again—to expand into something radiant. While Sam and I lived together, there was never room for me to become someone whose purpose strayed beyond making her feel more attractive by comparison. If looking toward my own exoskeleton had ever reminded her to soften, I no longer wanted to do this.

NEAR THE beginning of *The Descent of Man, and Selection in Relation to Sex,* Charles Darwin writes about a notch of flesh that occasionally appears on the human ear's helix. He goes on to deem it the vestige of a pointed ear long lost to most humans, though one still extant in other primates. This extra skin is now present in only a small percentage of the population, more in some nations and races than others, more commonly among Swedes and Native

Americans than Inuits for instance. What has become known as "Darwin's tubercle" still serves as evidence of our ongoing evolution. It tells us that as a species we are unfinished. Yet pointed ears in apes and monkeys continue funneling sound for survival deep within the forest. These animals have retained the ability to move their ears independently while the rest of their heads stay stationary. In this way, they can search for predators or prey in one direction while listening for them in the opposite.

I am among those humans who retain this atavism. The extra flesh at my ear's helix feels harder than the rest of the skin surrounding it, a small refusal to adapt to new environments looking ugly compared to the forest's lush foliage. Having only the remnant of a pointed ear, however, does not affect the sense of hearing. It serves no biological purpose among modern humans. All it does is to remind us that evolution has forced us to turn our heads in order to hear each other clearly. Whenever we neglect to look at someone who is speaking, we have a softer sense of hearing while missing their faces. We have a harder time discerning nuances in each other's voices when we fail to see eyes that also speak, when we fail to notice whether they fill with light or darken. Evolution has compelled us to look at each other for reasons beyond detecting predators or prey in the forest. Only the hardest part of my ear's helix sometimes forgets this.

A FEW months after she started community college, Sam called and told me she was coming back to Chicago to visit. I knew she expected me to look forward to this, to feel excitement even, but I told her no, she couldn't. I surprised myself with how curtly I said it. I told her this even though she never asked my permission to stay with me, even though I dreaded her reaction. She assumed I wasn't welcoming her into my new apartment because of Adam. She told me I was holding resentment, but I knew I was grateful to him, grateful for their relationship. Much as I might have once thought I almost loved him, he had given me a reason for not allowing Sam back into my life again, for keeping a space open. In her absence, beauty and ugliness became less oppressive forces as I swam more freely in between them, as I went to work and classes without any comments on the energy that was either flowing smoothly through my chakras or wasn't.

After I told her she would have to stay with someone else instead, she hung up the phone on me. Days later, I realized I wasn't angry but also had little desire to speak to her again, which made this our last conversation. I let Sam pass through me as if I were made of air alone, not a solid body, years before I began making this into a practice while walking among seas of nameless faces. She let go of our friendship with a similar ease, I imagined, because she also never reached out to me. That or she simply sensed a hardness, a second body she might have often glimpsed when we lived together, an exo-skeleton she knew she couldn't puncture when I heard only her voice over the phone and could not study her facial expressions.

When my mom had driven up and helped me move to a smaller apartment, she remarked on how few clothes I had, less than over the past several years she knew she bought me. I told her Sam had taken most of them, including all my favorites. She had worn my jeans and sweaters and blouses so often she probably felt she owned them. I had always assumed my mom liked Sam, admired her beauty the same as everyone else did. But when I told her she was moving, she surprised me by saying Sam would always do as she wanted. While knowing nothing about Adam, my mom had somehow sensed Sam made my life less free than I liked. My mom was also always looking into people's faces. She watched and listened, did both simultaneously.

Most of the time, I felt at ease in her looking, in her close observation. I sometimes imagined she saw more than she ever could have done in reality. I felt some part of her saw through to the life inside that pulses and evolves across species, from birds to primates, including humans. Had she never seen past all my beauty and ugliness, had she not somehow made me feel this without saying anything, I may also never have discovered my own ability to become less solid, lose some of the heaviness of my personality. If her simple act of looking hadn't made me aware of a certain endless depth I can fall down without ever hitting bottom, I may never have found courage to keep a space open while doing nothing more than walking in silence, looking into people's faces, trying to listen.

Amy's mom had been a nurse for as long as I could remember and still likely was one when I saw her daughter grocery shopping. She had visited our grammar school to check everyone in our class for head lice when I was six or seven. When my turn came, she ran the metal comb across my scalp as lightly as she had likely done with everyone else before me. I remember my nerves dissolving in near ecstasy, while I found her voice sibilant and soothing. Although Amy resembled her closely, I often privately wondered if her daughter was a disappointment. When Amy wiggled her ears for attention and I saw moist clumps of wax at their centers, filling her head's inner darkness, how clean, how very clean, I felt in comparison. That she could move them while keeping the rest of her head stationary seemed strange and primitive to me. This was long before I discovered an extra notch of skin at each ear's helix, before I realized our core softness transcends persons, transcends species.

Amy's mom's hair was visibly thinning in what must have been her early thirties. Amy's dad—I learned later from my own when he drove me to a slumber party at their farm for Amy's birthday—had declared bankruptcy a couple years ago. Although he continued farming, he had to do so at a smaller scale than all those around him. The few times I went to her house along with every other girl in my class, I saw few tractors, a dearth of barns and machinery. Although I thought her parents had poor taste in furniture and upholstery, although their house struck me as dark and lightless and I noticed their mantel went undusted, I also felt a core kindness in both her parents. Her dad didn't say much but smiled easily, always seemed a little embarrassed.

Amy lived as far from the town where we went to school as I did. She lived, though, in the opposite direction, so close to an airfield that we could hear small planes flying overhead from her living room and kitchen. A field for air alone, I thought to myself as Amy inevitably grew angry halfway through the party, as she stormed at her younger sister and the party split into factions and I had trouble sleeping. Throughout the little time I spent there, on only a few evenings during all of grammar school, I took solace in the field that was never planted with either corn or soybeans like all of those around it. I never saw the field or any of the planes for myself. Still I knew there was a place not far from this reserved solely for lifting heavy engines and cockpits into the sky's expanses. When I wanted to leave the slumber party early but knew I couldn't, I found this comforting. If Amy ever wanted to leave her life and board any of these airplanes herself, I never noticed.

I have difficulty picturing her mom and mine ever having a conversation, though they must have done so often, after plays and volleyball games and PTA conferences. Our grammar school was such a small one. I still have trouble pairing them in the same visual frame in my memory, perhaps because my mom filled our house with light and lightness, kept it clean to sparkling. Whereas Amy's left her mantel dusty. She could not keep her oldest daughter from wiggling her ears or throwing temper tantrums. My mom was naturally pretty if careless with her appearance, almost never wearing lipstick. While Amy's came to school from the hospital she worked in looking funny wearing makeup, with white pants too tight on her bottom. My mom's skin glowed golden even during winter, while that of Amy's mom was pockmarked with a flowering of scarlet. I cannot imagine either one being anything other than pleasant, giving each other all the space they needed. They must have known their daughters hardly interacted.

THAT I have recently begun walking in a conscious softness toward strangers is something I am aware makes no difference to anyone I'm passing. Keeping my mind empty takes almost all my concentration, too much for me to do anything else that might serve a purpose. I am not saying hello to anyone as I do this, am not even smiling. To find this place where death turns to life and where life turns to death again is all I'm hoping to gain by this. This place of transformation, this mystery we all inhabit, is still where I think I'm most likely to find my mom again, a place as far from an exoskeleton as can be imagined. A place where life begins to transition from something solid into something closer to air or liquid. A space of pure beauty then. I say this knowing no amount of walking among strangers free of judgment can ever rid me of instinctive aversions.

More than a decade ago, I sat with my dad in the cafeteria of the hospital where my mom was dying. He was eating off a plastic tray, and I was drinking a diet soft drink. All the food looked greasy, unhealthy in the extreme, though my dad seemed to enjoy the hamburger patty slathered with gravy, the buttered rolls that had been left all afternoon to harden beside the milk cartons. My mom had been sick for months by then. He hadn't had a hot meal in ages. He would never eat a decent one again, though at the time I doubt he thought of this. He was simply hungry. He gave me some quarters for the vending machine, urged me to buy something. The fact I realized this was a treat for him only made it more depressing.

I hadn't seen Amy's mom in more years than I could have said, but when she walked past where my dad and I were sitting, she looked the same to me. She looked just as rounded and as hairless as when she had ushered me inside a house feeling lightless as a basement during slumber parties. My dad didn't like her. Of this I felt certain. He had a perennially tough time liking women he found unattractive. I wondered if part of her sensed this, though she gave no indication she needed a space for beauty from him. She stayed standing at a small distance while we were sitting. No one hugged or touched each other's skin. If her eyes were brown or blue or green, I didn't notice.

She asked about my mom, and I told her the diagnosis. I remember being succinct about it. However rude I may have seemed, I also sensed my dad being grateful for me not dragging the conversation out any longer than needed. Where I trust my memory less concerns her reaction. I should probably take for granted her being sympathetic. Part of me believes she said how sorry she was and meant it. She must have said something anodyne, something expected. Only her face, the way she held her pale body as she towered above us, told me something different. I looked at her directly, saw something beyond whatever I heard her saying.

Maybe I still imagine it, but I felt a certain joy infuse her presence. I can still see a smile of her too brightly painted lips, an expansion of her face into a gentler roundness. Her tone, her gestures, her expression all conveyed an indulgence, a sense this was something that simply had to happen, perhaps because as a nurse she had seen the same so often. A woman once far prettier than she had ever been had started dying well before retirement. Then she said Amy was doing well without me asking. She added she worked in town at some nonprofit association, was head of human resources. She had a husband and a baby. I suppose I should have told her to pass on my congratulations, but I didn't. I thought we had left each other's lives already.

Amy's mom walked away then, took the elevator to see some patients as she sipped a cup of coffee. My dad shook his head at her large stomach and bottom. He finished the last of his hamburger patty and mentioned she had recently gotten a promotion. He had read in the newspaper she was now head of all the nurses. He said he couldn't imagine making the money she was bringing in while healthcare costs kept rising. Every day in the hospital cost a small fortune. His fear that it could bankrupt him was genuine.

A SPACE, if not for beauty then for becoming something different than she seemed and had always been. Neither one of us could give this to someone we had no reason for disliking but did anyway at the moment. Whatever lay behind the lightness I sensed in a woman whose first name I have either never known or have long forgotten, I ascribe all our callousness—my dad and mine and this woman's included—to the hardness of the living, the hardness that seems to go with having a body that still functions, still seems self-sufficient, a vehicle for independence. Softening for me has been far from a natural process. Had life gone more as I wanted, I believe I would have been more tempted to continue hardening without any awareness, a little more each year without knowing until I turned to stone entirely. I would have continued becoming more of the person I was already becoming before absence created so much space, so much emptiness. Maybe it is only the dying who know what it is to truly soften. To die is to become spacious to the point another person can walk through you and never know it. Maybe this is really what I'm doing, how I'm still coping. Dying while living.

Yesterday while I was walking to the grocery store near my apartment, I confronted a mound of strawberries spilled across the sidewalk. A whole carton had been wasted as a plane flew closely overhead. Bodies invisible to me looked out small windows and erased part of the sky's emptiness. Many were likely talking to those seated beside them, looking forward to landing, wondering about catching their connections. But I could neither hear nor see them as an ambulance rushed past, screaming in panic. I walked inside the same grocery store I visit every week, and no one knew me. I bought milk and bread then stepped outside the door again. To anyone inside who may have been watching, I vanished. The sidewalk was crowded, but everyone made space enough for me to pass them. I looked toward the skyline. Fields of air spread before me.

THANKS

I have difficulty tracing my interest in vestigial organs back to its origins, but I remain grateful to my husband, Robert, for never questioning this as a valid field of inquiry and for being supportive of my writing endeavors, in general, however little sense they may make on the surface. The same goes for my sister, Melanie, who has always afforded me ample leeway to be myself, both on and off the page, as well as to invoke my own, subjective memories of our parents. Extremely huge thanks too to everyone at Autumn House Press, especially Mike Good, my editor, whose careful reading, literary sensitivity, and generous spirit helped bring each essay into its final form. While writing this book, I had every reason to doubt it would ever be published, so my gratitude also goes out to those editors of the literary magazines where some of these essays first appeared in slightly different versions and thus for giving me encouragement along the way. Finally, I want to offer immense thanks to Paul Lisicky for finding something in these essays that resonated. The word "vestigial" for me primarily conjures the feeling of being left behind, and so to be included in the literary community through these pages means a great deal.

ACKNOWLEDGMENTS

"Cloud Elephants" first appeared in *TINGE Magazine.*

"The End of Longing" first appeared in *American Literary Review.*

"Ghost Feet" first appeared in the *Nashville Review.*

"The Mermaids of Austin" first appeared in *Terrain.org.*

"Nurturing Instincts" first appeared in *Entropy.*

"Running through Water" first appeared in *The Rumpus.*

"Skull Cathedral" first appeared in *The Collapsar.*

"Swallowing Needles" first appeared in *Phoebe.*

"A Traveling Circus" first appeared in *Noble / Gas Qtrly.*

"Man in the Moon" first appeared in *Waxwing.*

"Winter Honey" first appeared in *Hot Metal Bridge.*